Praise for
Suzanne Jessee's Escape Anxiety Program

"If you have the desire to change your life and rebirth yourself free of your old emotional afflictions, this program will coach and guide you in ways, which will allow you to escape your past and its destructive messages."

Bernie Siegel, MD
Author of *365 Prescriptions for the Soul, Prescriptions for Living*
and *Love, Medicine and Miracles*

"Suzanne Jessee has written an informative and instructional book on the 'How's and Why's' of using meditation-based therapies to 'Escape Anxiety.'

The therapeutic value of these practices and the practical steps she gives in this book guide the reader toward a modicum of self-control over the anxiety and panic that plagues them.

I congratulate and honor her effort to bring this information to all who suffer in a most useable and simplified system."

Harry L. Haroutunian, MD
Physician Director, Betty Ford Center, a part of the Hazelden Betty Ford

"Escape Anxiety is a powerful program that will help many people calm the worry and stress that steals their joy."

Dr. Daniel Amen
Amen Clinics, Inc.
Author of *Change Your Brain, Change Your Body*

"Think of Suzanne as a scout, or the one who 'goes before' you, as one who marks the path to follow toward freedom and light. If you dive into this book, immerse yourself in the story, try out the tools, and incorporate the principles into your own life, you will find safety, healing, freedom and peace."

Lavelle Jacobson, Master of Divinity
Spiritual Care Counselor
Betty Ford Center, a part of the Hazelden Betty Ford Foundation

"Some years ago during a business trip, I was caught in the cross gun-fire between two gangs. It left me dealing with anxiety attacks. I tried ignoring them and hoping they would go away and realized that this was getting worse and must be resolved.

Doctors were some help, but most of the work needed to be done by the person burdened by the attacks. I found Suzanne's meditation tapes very helpful and would carry them with me even when I traveled. They were a vital tool for my journey of recovery and are still used when I have a stressful day."

Wanda
Victim of a violent crime

"The Escape Anxiety program has literally changed my life. It's the driving tool that fine-tunes the mind to allow one to accomplish goals. The program has given me the mental power to release the stress in my life. Through Suzanne's techniques, I can now clearly see and set aside the negative aspects that were once driving my life. The Escape Anxiety program has literally transformed me. It has allowed me to lose 15 pounds and focus on eating healthier and smarter. But most importantly, it has allowed me to respect and love myself. This in turn has brought those that are dearest to me closer. I owe a life of gratitude to Suzanne Jessee's program."

Cameron Fraide
Palm Desert, California

Escape Anxiety

8 Steps to Freedom
Through Meditative Therapies

Suzanne Jessee, M.A., C.Ht.

SelectBooks, Inc.
New York

Neurogenesis Meditative Therapy™ (NMT) is a trademark of Suzanne Jessee

This edition published by SelectBooks, Inc.
For information address SelectBooks, Inc., New York, New York.

First Edition

ISBN 978-1-59079-301-5

Library of Congress Cataloging-in-Publication Data
Jessee, Suzanne.
  Escape anxiety : 8 steps to freedom through meditative therapies / Suzanne Jessee, M.A., CHt. -- First Edition.
      pages cm
  Includes bibliographical references and index.
  Summary: "Author presents her 8-Step Escape Anxiety program, used at the Betty Ford Center and other treatment facilities, developed after her own experience of hospitalization for anxiety disorders and related alcoholism. Program is based on her concept of Neurogenesis Meditative Therapy (NMT) that integrates practices of progressive relaxation, mindfulness meditation, guided imagery meditation, hypnotherapy, and cognitive behavioral therapy"-- Provided by publisher.
  ISBN 978-1-59079-301-5 (hardbound book : alk. paper) 1. Anxiety. 2. Anxiety--Treatment. 3. Meditation. I. Title.
  BF575.A6.J47 2015
  152.4'6--dc23
                              2014037642

Book design by Janice Benight
Book illustrations by Lidiya Matvisiv
Spot illustrations © istockphoto/Helga Wigandt

Manufactured in the United States of America
10 9 8 7 6 5 4 3 2 1

This is a continuation of the copyright page.

To all of the beloved children:
Jason, Breanna, Sarah, Amber, Amanda, Stephanie,
and Baby Girl born 8/24/77,
whose delicate lives God entrusted to me.
To my grandchildren, now and to come,
with my deepest love.

Manifest your dreams!

Contents

Part II
Eight Steps to Freedom:
The Escape Anxiety Program 69

CHAPTER FOUR
Step 1: Conquering Codependent Control Issues   71

CHAPTER FIVE
Step 2: Dismantling Perfectionism   91

Foreword

There are times in life when we need something, anything, to get us through. And there are times in life that we're doing okay, but need that extra sparkle of inspiration to add some dazzle to our daily lives. No matter where you are coming from, or why you picked up this book, you are guaranteed to find some light and inspiration here.

This is not just a "how to" book, but a story, a journey with Suzanne as she shares her life story and the transformation that she experienced from the darkness of anxiety to freedom and light. Better than fiction, Suzanne tells her story with heart, always sharing her profound wisdom, the tools she has learned, her expertise as a clinical counselor and the hope she has experienced and brings to you, the reader.

Suzanne came into my life at a crucial time. Struggling with major life-altering decisions, a stressful yet rewarding career, overwhelming transitions in my home life, and significant grief and loss, Suzanne's friendship was steady, present, consistent, and deep. When I think of Suzanne, these are a few of the things that come to my mind: breath of fresh air. Cool water on a hot afternoon. Rest when weary. Light in darkness. Lighthearted yet not one to skim the surface, Suzanne was a safe haven of friendship where I could be real, yet not be left to despair.

You will find *Escape Anxiety* to be the same. Lighthearted yet not superficial, safe but not boring, real but not melancholy.

As a friend and colleague, Suzanne saw my anxiety and slipped me one of her meditation CD sets. I began to use it daily, giving myself the much-needed break and rejuvenation. And slowly things began to change. I felt lighter, more centered, more able to surrender the uncontrollable aspects of my life and trust rather than live in worry and anxiety. It felt like a spa for my soul. I had found a tool to help with life, or rather, *stressful* life. (Oh, you have one of those too?) Suzanne's meditations led me to a peaceful place each day, giving me the serenity, connection to my own spirituality, an ability to let go of heavy things, and the rejuvenation and strength I needed for the day.

As a Spiritual Care Counselor at the Betty Ford Center, I knew this had to be shared. With her permission, I began using Suzanne's meditations with the addicted and alcoholic women on my hall at Betty Ford Center. Each time I did, their response was "Where do we get those meditations? We want those for when we get home!" The meditations are non-religious (and not weird and woo-woo-ey at all!) but rather are grounded in deep spirituality, inspired by the beauty of nature and principles of goodness and truth. Therefore, they are perfect for people from any religious or cultural background.

Suzanne's journey was not easy. And my guess is that yours is not either. So think of Suzanne as a scout, or the one who "goes before" you, as one who marks the path to follow toward freedom and light. (Not blindly, of course, because that's not good for anyone.) If you dive into this book, immerse yourself in the story, try out the tools, and incorporate the principles into your own life, you will find safety, healing, freedom, and peace.

—Lavelle Jacobson, Master of Divinity
Spiritual Care Counselor
Betty Ford Center,
A part of the Hazelden Betty Ford Foundation

Acknowledgments

I want to thank a few special friends and my beloved family for being the wind beneath my wings in manifesting my dreams.

I want to thank God for giving me a peace of mind beyond all understanding, for inspiring my purpose and vision, and for planting in me an insatiable drive to guide others to peace of mind. Along my journey, I have often made many appointments for one purpose but discovered that God had an entirely different plan for these meetings. God planted very special people in these meetings who became my unintentional dream-makers—I call these meetings "divine appointments."

Thank you Mike Hammer for your generous contribution to my plan and purpose. It is with your belief in me that my dream has taken flight. You were a divine appointment!

My deepest gratitude goes to my dear friend since childhood, Kerre Randel—a witness to my life, an encourager, supporter, contributor, and believer in my quest to share my story of struggle and triumph for the greater good.

My son Jason, at the tender age of eleven, had the courage to be the mirror to my broken reflection. My life was forever changed in that moment. Thank you, my dear loving son.

My daughter Breanna encouraged me to never lose my sight of my dream, ever nudging me forward. "Go forward mom, don't give up, you've got this" she would say to me on our frequent hikes up the San Jacinto Mountains. Thank you, my beautiful love.

Ellen Daly, you are gifted beyond measure. Thank you for giving my words a voice with flow in print. I thank God for the divine appointment with Mike Murphy that brought me to you so that we could bring this work to all those who will benefit from it, with ease and grace.

The first moment I heard the soothing, spiritual music of Mark Watson, I knew I had been divinely appointed to share the private meditations of my mind within the melodic language of his sounds. This collaboration has been essential to the development of this work.

I also want to express my deep appreciation to my publisher and editor, who took a chance on me with time limitations that most publishers would not have been willing to work within. I'm forever grateful for the divine appointment with Joel Pitney, who initiated this fortuitous partnership.

To my patients, thank you for trusting in me to gently guide your frail and vulnerable minds to a place of peace, hope, and renewal. It was your peace-filled faces and grateful voices that affirmed my purpose in life. I am forever grateful.

Finally, to my mom and dad, thank you for allowing me to share the story of our journey unfiltered and for giving me perfect love. We are perfectly imperfect! All my love to you both.

Introduction

In 1991, just shy of my thirtieth birthday, I was hospitalized with severe depression, anxiety, panic disorder, and the early stages of agoraphobia (fear of going out in public). If you'd told me back then, as I stood shaking uncontrollably in my kitchen, that one day I'd be writing a book to help anxiety sufferers, or that I'd train and work at some of the leading recovery centers in the country as a clinical therapist, I'd have thought you were crazy. Because, after all, that's what I was: crazy. So crazy I couldn't even leave the house. Anyone telling me I'd be making anything of my life must be crazy too. At that moment, all I could see ahead was a life incarcerated in a psych ward. I even wondered if I'd have a life at all.

When I realized I would survive the incapacitating effects of panic disorder, it became my life's passion to understand the nature of anxiety and panic attacks from a physiological and psychological perspective. I wanted to understand why I became so ill in a fairly short period of time, and make sure that I would never experience that degree of mental distress again. With a passion for my personal wellness as the catalyst for my mission, I set out to study, train, and work in the world's leading hospitals, treatment centers, and educational institutions.

More than two decades later, I look back in amazement and gratitude at how far I've come. In my own journey of recovery from anxiety and the alcoholism I developed through attempting to self-medicate, I discovered tools that were so powerful I felt compelled to share them with others. These tools are not new—in fact, some of them have been around for thousands of years. But only recently has the medical community come to understand the effectiveness of these therapies for treating anxiety. And thanks to advances in science, we can now not only witness their effectiveness, but can study the physical evidence of their impact on our brains and bodies.

I have seamlessly woven the most effective therapies for treating anxiety—which include Progressive Relaxation; Mindfulness Meditation; Guided Imagery Meditation; Hypnosis and Hypnotherapy; and Cognitive Behavioral Therapy—into a new powerful treatment for recovery from anxiety disorders, which I call Neurogenesis Meditative Therapy™ (NMT). NMT is a form of guided meditation that is the central treatment in my 8-Step Escape Anxiety Program, which I've used at leading recovery centers, including the Betty Ford Center, Brighton Hospital, and Dawn Farms Treatment Center.

The Escape Anxiety Program, which I am unveiling for the first time in this book, is the culmination of my clinical understanding of panic disorder paired with the absolute best alternative-healing methods known to science for the reversal and prevention of panic disorder. Now, through this book, I'm thrilled to be able to make this program available to tens of thousands more sufferers—people who may not be able to afford expensive recovery centers, or may be too ashamed or confused to seek treatment.

I believe that in our ever-more-stressful culture, it's critical to help people understand anxiety and remove its cloak of shame. It's estimated that forty million Americans suffer from this disorder. My mission in life is to make excellent mental healthcare affordable and accessible to anyone who needs it, in the comfort of their own homes.

If you've picked up this book, perhaps you are one of those people. Or perhaps someone you know and love is suffering the agony of anxiety, and you are seeking to help him or her. Whether you are a long-term sufferer with an advanced anxiety disorder, a concerned friend seeking help for a loved one, or simply someone who has suffered an occasional panic attack and wants to prevent it escalating into something more serious, I can help you. In fact, the tools in this book are relevant for anywho lives a high-stress lifestyle, which most of us do. Prevention is by far the best medicine, and I hope this book will prove useful not just as a responsive treatment but as a preventative treatment as well, helping to avert the spiral into an anxiety disorder for many.

In part I, I will share my own story of breakdown and recovery, as well as the stories of my patients (with names and identities changed to protect privacy), and use these to highlight and demystify the causes and symptoms of the disorder. In part II, I will be walking you through my proven 8-Step Escape Anxiety Program, giving you tools and techniques to manage your condition and find freedom from its devastating consequences, such as addiction, depression, and more. At the end of this book, I also include vital information about nutrition, exercise, and the dangers of substance abuse. Knowledge is power, so I encourage you to spend time reading through this information, as it will help you to manage your own symptoms more effectively through smart lifestyle choices.

The overall objective of the exercises in the 8 steps in the Escape Anxiety program is to take a close look at the contributing factors to your anxiety and panic disorder. Those factors may include, but are not limited to, control issues, perfectionism, resentment, anger and guilt, catastrophic thinking, low self-esteem, and negative self-talk. All of these elements are rooted in deep-seated fear that creates unmanageable stress resulting in chronic anxiety and panic attacks.

As we work through the 8 steps, we will do some mental reorganizing and de-cluttering by throwing out the old and bringing in the new—purging negative energy and replacing it with positive, healthy energy. Each step addresses specific emotional contributors to anxiety and panic disorder.

Take as much time as you need to work through the 8 steps in the program. Each of the steps in part II includes exercises and a specially designed guide for meditation called a Neurogenesis Meditative Therapy script. If you find yourself struggling with any particular step, I encourage you to stay with it and repeat the exercises until you feel confident you have fully absorbed the ideas and practices. And please don't stress over trying to complete this program within a designated time frame—you have enough stress already. Escape Anxiety is a powerfully effective program, but it was also designed to be enjoyable. Relax and take it easy. It's a journey and I'm with you all the way.

Remember, this is a program of progress, not perfection. Be easy on yourself. Although you should find some immediate relief, long-term healing is a process. Allow yourself to feel whatever you feel. Give yourself well-earned credit for beginning this life-altering program, and being an active participant in your own recovery. Throughout the various exercises, I will remind you to be responsible for your part in your physical, emotional, and spiritual state of being and healing. We can't change what we fail to acknowledge.

As we progress through this journey, I will occasionally make references to God. I believe that faith in a higher power, whatever that higher power may be for you, is essential in recovery. But if you are not comfortable with traditional ideas of God, I want to suggest that you substitute whatever is meaningful to you—it might be "the Universe," "the Divine Light," "the Mystery," or any number of variations. I encourage you to use your own understanding of God according to your personal beliefs.

The application of spiritual principles is a staple feature of this program. Religion, in all its forms, supports and teaches these simple yet powerful principles for abundant living that have stood the test of time. Spirituality is also a component of the medical model of wellness. For me to disregard the spiritual element would be professionally unethical. However, this is not a religious program and does not require you to adopt any particular belief system. It is a medically sound program with spiritual principles. You will be able to easily adapt these concepts to your daily life regardless of your personal religious preferences, or even if you don't have a religious preference.

Finally, please note that the Escape Anxiety program is not intended for the diagnosis of any medical condition. Symptoms of anxiety and panic may be related to a more serious medical condition. Please consult with a professional to determine if you need medical intervention. This program is not intended to be a substitute for medication or psychiatric or psychological therapies. Ask your doctor or therapist about incorporating this program into your existing course of treatment. Seek immediate help if you are exhibiting symptoms that may threaten your health, including but not limited to persistent insomnia, dramatic mood changes, or thoughts of suicide.

Writing this book has been a major milestone for me. It is my testimony that recovery from the debilitating effects of anxiety disorder and mental illness is real, and dreams do come true when we choose to follow them, despite our genetic inheritances and unfortunate life circumstances. Today, I am free from the bondage of anxiety and panic disorder. I am delighted and honored that you have chosen me to be your guide and personal thought trainer on this journey. Together we will combine forces and travel out of the captivity of panic and fear and into emotional freedom and peace of mind.

—SUZANNE JESSEE
Palm Desert, California, November 2014

Escape Anxiety

Part I

DECODING ANXIETY DISORDERS

Freaking Out!
Anatomy of a Panic Attack

*I have come to believe that anxiety accompanies intellectual
activity as its shadow, and that the more we know of the
nature of anxiety, the more we will know of intellect.*

—Howard Liddell, PhD
"The Role of Vigilance in the Development of Animal Neurosis"

The double doors looked like the doors of any other clinic. As I paused on the top step, my reflection stared back at me from the glass, shadowy but familiar. Yet I knew that I was stepping into a place unlike any I'd ever been before, and I would not come out the same. I was about to check myself in to a psychiatric hospital.

That day in 1991 had begun like most other days at that point in my life: in a blind panic. As the dawn light penetrated my consciousness, so did the now-familiar sensation of desperation and despair that had been greeting me every morning for the past three months. I lay as if paralyzed, my body and nerves exposed and awash with a sense of inevitable, impending doom. Deep sadness and hopeless accompanied the fear. These feelings were now my constant companions. They persisted despite my attempts to pretend them away, drink them away, distract them away, and pray them away. Nothing, absolutely nothing, could relieve my ever-growing mental anguish. I had lost control of my emotions.

I was no stranger to mental illness. I'd watched my aunt descend into schizophrenia, and knew that a great-aunt who ironically shared my name and birth date had spent the better part of her life in mental institutions. This is it, I thought, as I lay in bed. This is my destiny. I am mentally ill. My fear spiraled into deepening panic. I am mentally ill. I will live the rest of my life in a mental institution, locked up like a caged animal, in a dim, grim, dark hell! I began to sweat. I wanted to throw up, but I was afraid that if I did I would never stop, that my body would just continue to retch until I would die. I wanted to run, to get away from my thoughts, my reality, my today, my tomorrow, my forever, my fear of me, my mind, and my life. But I couldn't run, because there it would be. It was inside of me. It was in my head and I desperately wanted it to stop, to leave me alone.

I wanted to run somewhere, but I needed to rest. I couldn't go anywhere, anyway, because I was afraid to go outside. I couldn't seem to catch my breath. I wanted a hug but didn't want anyone to touch me. Nobody could possibly understand what I was going through. The thought of someone comforting me made me feel even more hopeless because I knew that no one I knew could help me. Not even my mother, who always provided some comfort or words of wisdom to give me hope. I felt no hope. The walls were closing in on me. This was my worst nightmare and I was wide-awake. In fact, it felt like the moment you first wake up from a horrifying nightmare and every cell in your body is bursting with terror. That is what I was feeling, but it wasn't a nightmare. It was my very real mental hell.

I leapt out of bed, as if my mind was chasing me, and ran into the kitchen. In a state of full-blown terror, I threw open the door of the nearest cupboard and grabbed a can of vegetables as if grabbing for a life raft in the midst of raging storm in a vast sea. Through the fog of panic, I began to read the labels, between my gasps for air and repressed tears. I knew that if I allowed myself to cry, I would never stop—that my cries would turn to screams and I would fall off the fragile raft of sanity to which I was desperately clinging. The letters blurred before my eyes, but I fought for focus. "If I can just focus on these words and know what they mean, then I can check to see if I still have some sanity," I told myself.

"Green beans. They grow in fields. They're green and long and have a seam with a string. We eat them for nutrition. I don't like them but they are good for me." Deep breath. "Salt. Salt makes green beans taste better, but too much is not good. I like the flavor of salt." I grabbed another can. "Corn. Corn is yellow. It grows on a stalk." I went on reading food can labels until finally my panic began to subside. Tomatoes. Peas. Black beans. Sitting on my kitchen floor, I thought about what they tasted like, felt like, looked like.

I knew, as I put the last can down, that I had lost the fight. I had to get help. The phone rang. It was my Dad, concern evident in his voice as he asked,

"Honey, are you okay?"

"No, Dad, I'm not okay."

"Your mother and I think you may need to go to the hospital. Would you like for me to take you to the hospital?"

I said yes. "Yes, I would."

Immediately, I felt some relief, married with the deepest sadness I had ever known. That's how bad things had gotten—so bad that the idea of a psychiatric hospital felt like relief. And the only thing I knew about psychiatric hospitals was what I had seen in *One Flew Over the Cuckoo's Nest*. That's right, that's what I voluntarily signed up for. Straitjacket anyone? Yeah, me, please—I'll take one of those.

I didn't know what I would face and for how long, but I knew I was very sick and I couldn't go on like this. I had an eighteen-month-old baby, I had just started a new job, and I was the primary earner in my household. What was going to happen to my baby, my home, my finances, my marriage, or my brand new job that was keeping us afloat? I couldn't afford to be sick or take time off to get help. What would people say? What would I tell people? I couldn't tell anyone that I'd literally lost my mind! I would never be able to go back to work and face my co-workers. A heavy coat of shame washed over me, which faded into truth. None of this mattered anymore. I couldn't manage any of this. I was in a state of complete surrender.

As I stood outside those glass doors at Millwood Hospital in Arlington, Texas, I thought to myself, "God has really abandoned me now." I looked at my reflection again. Where was she, the young woman who had had so much ambition, drive, and determination? The capable, responsible mother deeply in love with her two children? The professional with goals to move into management and maybe even training? All of these had been reduced to the skeletal figure looking back at me, her face furrowed with mental anguish and desperation, weighing barely 104 pounds. She was hardly recognizable as the woman I had been just three short months ago.

"Where was God?" I asked myself. "Why did he let this happen to me? I thought was going to have a life of purpose, and yet now I stand at the doorway of a psychiatric hospital. This is the darkest day of my life." I opened the door and stepped inside.

A few days later, I was eagerly awaiting my first visit with my assigned psychiatrist. By this time I had settled in. The hospital was nice; the nurses were friendly. No one had offered me a straitjacket or proposed electric shock therapy. I hadn't seen anyone in a hospital gown shuffling down the hallway drooling—only a group of chatty patients on their way to the gym for a game of volleyball. I was beginning to feel some hope, along with a healthy need to know what in the hell happened to me. I was anxious to see the doctor because I was sure he was going to give me an explanation and set me on the road to recovery.

Well, that didn't turn out quite as planned. When I asked him what had happened to me—how I could have gone so quickly from being a high-functioning sales rep, mother, and wife to being a basket case who couldn't get out of bed in the morning—he just gave me a blank stare. I couldn't tell if he was thinking "You're kidding me, right? I'm here to treat you, not educate you!" or "Do you really think I need to tell you all the reasons you ended up here?" or maybe just, "I don't know how to tell you what happened to you because it has never happened to me." Whatever his thoughts or reasons, he promptly proceeded to write me a prescription for the latest and greatest psychotropic medication, and that was the end of our consultation.

Understanding Anxiety

I left that doctor's office frustrated, but still determined to come to a clear understanding as to how a normal person could descend into a debilitating mental illness in what appeared to be a matter of months. And if the doctor wasn't going to or wasn't able to give it to me, I would have to get it myself. For me, it was not enough just to start feeling better. I needed to know why I felt bad in the first place, and how I could prevent it happening again. I've always lived by the old adage that "knowledge is power," and the doctor's lack of explanations left me feeling helpless. I sensed intuitively that there was something I had missed along the road of life, some tool or skill or warning that could have prevented this from becoming such a catastrophe. And I was determined to find out what it was so it would never catch me by surprise again. This journey of understanding would take me the next twenty years of my life.

All I knew at that point was that I had an "anxiety disorder" and that my experience that morning with the vegetable cans was a full-blown panic attack. I quickly realized that this was not my first—I had already had several similar episodes. Thinking back over these events, it became clear that they were progressive in nature. Every time I had one, it was more intense and more disturbing than the last, and always followed by a deeper sense of shame.

As I began to read about this condition, I discovered some illuminating facts. One of the most surprising things I found was that anxiety as a disorder was not recognized in the medical community, and did not appear in the *Diagnostic and Statistical Manual of Mental Disorders* (the "bible" of mental health, published by the American Psychiatric Association), until its third edition in 1980, right after a new class of drugs hit the market to specifically treat anxiety. This means that the medicinal treatment for anxiety pre-dated professional acknowledgment of anxiety as a clinical mental health disorder. No wonder my doctor in 1991 couldn't give me much insight into my condition! He probably barely understood it himself.

The term Anxiety Disorder, I learned, is an umbrella term for a large number of disorders in which the primary feature is abnormal or inappropriate anxiety. Everybody has experienced anxiety at some point. Think about the last time you went for a job interview. Remember the feelings inside your body as you waited nervously outside the interview room. Chances are you experienced some of the common symptoms of anxiety like increased heart rate and tensed muscles. You may have noticed an intensity of focus and even a sense of impending doom. These are all normal symptoms of anxiety.

These symptoms only become a problem when they occur without any particular reason to feel threatened. When this occurs repeatedly, normal anxiety could be turning into an anxiety disorder. Here is an abbreviated list of the most common anxiety disorders. There are many more, but this will give you an idea of the different types.

Common Anxiety Disorders

- *Panic Disorder*—This disorder affects over six million Americans today, and is characterized by sudden and unexplained panic attacks. These attacks usually last around ten minutes, and can manifest in symptoms such as heart palpitations, weakness, difficulty breathing, fainting, dizziness, and sweating.

- *Obsessive-Compulsive Disorder*—This disorder affects over two million Americans, and often comes paired with other anxiety disorders, depression, specific phobias, and eating disorders. Sufferers of OCD most often have repeated thoughts or feelings without their control, or are compelled to perform certain actions against their will.

- *Post-Traumatic Stress Disorder*—This disorder affects over seven million Americans today and can arise at any time after a traumatic experience. PTSD often coexists with other anxiety disorders, or with depression or substance abuse.

- *Social Anxiety Disorder*—This disorder affects over one million Americans at any given time and is one of the most commonly reported anxiety disorders. It is characterized by intense, often debilitating fear in social situations, and can disrupt or completely prevent the sufferer from having normal social interactions.

- *Specific Phobias*—This disorder affects over nineteen million American adults and causes persistent and often irrational fear of certain objects or situations. These feelings of fear can greatly impair the life of the sufferer, forcing these persons to avoid certain locations or situations, and hindering their ability to exist peacefully with their surroundings.

☙ *Generalized Anxiety Disorder*—This disorder affects over six million Americans and is characterized by persistent and uncontrollable feelings of worry or anxiety without cause, or disproportionate feelings of worry over simple issues.

In this book I will be focusing on the general experience of anxiety symptoms and specifically their expression as panic attacks, but if you suffer from other specific forms as listed above, much of what I will be sharing will be equally relevant. Take the short quiz below to help you assess your own experience of anxiety.

QUIZ: Anxiety Self-Assessment

To help you recognize whether you may be experiencing symptoms of anxiety, answer Yes or No to the following questions:

1. Do you experience shortness of breath, heart palpitation, or shaking while at rest?

2. Do you have a fear of losing control or going crazy?

3. Do you avoid social situations because of fear?

4. Do you find that you need a drink or drug to participate in social events?

5. Do you have fears of specific objects?

6. Do you fear that you will be in a place or situation from which you cannot escape?

7. Do you feel afraid of leaving your home?

8. Do you have recurrent thoughts or images that disturb you and won't go away?

9. Do you persistently relive an upsetting event from the past?

Answering "yes" to more than four of these questions may indicate a problem with anxiety and the possible need to consult with a professional.

PLEASE NOTE: *This test is not intended to diagnose an illness; it is a tool to increase your awareness of your level of anxiety. If you feel that certain symptoms, such as those described above, are impacting your quality of life, the first step is to determine if there is an underlying medical condition that is causing the anxiety. Please seek the advice and support of a qualified healthcare professional to work with you.*

Anatomy of a Panic Attack

Let's take a closer look at what a panic attack is. According to the leading hospital Mayo Clinic, a panic attack is "a sudden episode of intense fear that triggers severe physical reactions when there is no real danger or apparent cause."[1] Does that sound familiar? Do you have episodes where you feel like you're losing control or having a heart attack? Do you find yourself irrationally paralyzed by terror, unable to control the spiraling anxiety that threatens to suck you into a black hole of your worst fears? If this happens to you repeatedly, you may be suffering from a Panic Disorder. The Mayo Clinic states that panic attacks typically include a few or many of these symptoms:

☙ Sense of impending doom or danger

☙ Fear of loss of control or death

☙ Rapid heart rate

☙ Sweating

☙ Trembling

☙ Shortness of breath

☙ Hyperventilation

☙ Chills

☙ Hot flashes

☙ Nausea

☙ Abdominal cramping

☙ Chest pain

☙ Headache

☙ Dizziness

☙ Faintness

☙ Tightness in your throat

☙ Trouble swallowing

One patient of mine her described her panic attacks as feeling like an elephant sitting on her chest. Her chest was tight and heavy and she couldn't seem to get a full breath. Another patient admits to frequenting the emergency room and regularly seeking out specialists with the latest technology in scanning and diagnosing to finally confirm her greatest fear that she has a heart problem, even though she has been told repeatedly that her symptoms are stress and anxiety-related panic attacks. A common denominator with every patient I have treated is they all feel like they are going to freak out or lose control.

Dan Harris, an ABC news anchor who suffered a panic attack live on air in front of five million people and later wrote a book about it, describes the physical experience vividly:

Out of nowhere, I felt like I was being stabbed in the brain with raw animal fear. A paralytic wave of panic rolled up through my shoulders, over the top of my head, then melted down the front of my face. The universe was collapsing on me. My heart started to gallop. My mouth dried up. My palms oozed sweat.[2]

If you, or someone you know, suffers from some combination of the symptoms I've been describing, you're not alone. In fact, I was amazed to discover how common this kind of experience was. Did you know that forty million American adults suffer from anxiety disorders, making them the most common mental illness in the United States? That means one in seven of us. An article published in the *American Journal of Psychiatry* in 2006 reports that Americans suffering with anxiety were losing an astounding 321 million days of work a year, which translated to $50 billion tab for the economy annually.[3] Given that anxiety seems to have been on the rise since then, just imagine what those figures might be today! Americans are not the only ones suffering, by the way. *The Canadian Journal of Psychiatry* estimated that worldwide, as many as one in six people will suffer from an anxiety disorder for at least a year at some point in their lifetimes.[4] And the statistics only account for those who identify the problem—there are millions more "silent sufferers" who are too confused or ashamed to seek professional help.

Feelings of shame: we should probably add that to the list of symptoms, as it seems to go hand in hand with panic attacks. It's confusing and embarrassing to find yourself terrified for no apparent reason. But you know what? Panic attacks are nothing to be ashamed of—they are actually your body doing its job!

Here's the good news: Our minds and bodies are designed to have anxiety and panic attacks for a reason. We panic because something in our world feels threatening to us. When we have that sense of fear, our brains respond with a chemical reaction designed to help us survive in a dangerous situation. This is a very good thing! Imagine if you were walking down the street in your neighborhood, enjoying a leisurely stroll when, all of a sudden out of nowhere, you found yourself the target of a very large, angry, snarling dog. If you had no mental or physical reaction to a situation like this at all, guess what you could be? Lunch!

In fact, your body is designed to respond instantaneously to threats like this by activating what Harvard psychologist Walter Cannon dubbed the "fight or flight" response. Cannon was the first to recognize, in 1915, that under threat the body reacts in a way that gives it the ability to fight harder or run faster in the event of imminent danger. I'm sure you've heard stories of average-sized men and women who find they can perform superhuman feats when they or their children are threatened. In a nutshell, this is how it works: You see danger, and your sympathetic nervous system immediately responds by stimulating the adrenal glands, triggering a surge of two primary chemicals known as stress hormones, cortisol and adrenaline. When these chemicals are released they travel with lightning speed throughout the central nervous system, enabling you to respond with far greater strength and speed for a brief period of time in order to survive. Pretty amazing, right?

The bad news, however, is that we can experience this same reaction *whether the threat is real or imagined*. In the mid-twentieth century, Hans Selye discovered that the amazing chain of physiological events that make up the "fight or flight" response can be triggered even if the threat is only in the mind. You can be sitting behind your desk, staring into the distance, and begin to daydream about an angry dog charging at you. Without realizing it, you have just engaged the very same part of your brain and caused the very same power-packed chemical reaction to be released, traveling all throughout your central nervous system and giving you super-human life-saving strength, without ever leaving the safety of your office.

That's powerful stuff. In its more intense forms, it can feel like you're having a heart attack, or you're literally about to die. The reality is, you aren't going to die, and you will recover. However, returning to a normal physical state may take a while—it varies depending on a person's ability to self-regulate (which we'll be learning more about in a later chapter), but can take up to sixty minutes for some.

Essentially, what I've just described is what occurs when you have a panic attack. Something in your mind sends a signal to your body that it's under threat, and your body responds exactly as it's been designed to do. If you look at the panic attack symptoms listed above, they're very similar to the physiological changes the body undergoes when it's getting ready to run or do battle. The problem is, there's nothing for you to fight or run from. As the Mayo Clinic definition said, a panic attack "triggers severe physical reactions *when there is no real danger or apparent cause.*"

Why Do We Panic When There's Nothing to Panic About?

So are people who suffer from panic attacks just victims of their own imaginations? Well, not entirely. The truth is a little more complex than that. Our bodies are responding to *something*—just not the thing they were designed to respond to.

Let's think, for a moment, about the circumstances under which the "fight or flight" mechanism evolved. Our earliest ancestors lived in a world where they faced daily physical threats and sources of stress like wolves and bears, marauding tribes, or natural disasters. They desperately needed those power-packed hormones to help them survive. Fast-forward to today's world, and most of us face stressors that are inherently different than those faced by our ancestors.

Triggers
   1. Sound
   2. Sight
   3. Smell
   4. Touch/Feel

Brain Responses
   a) Amygdala (emotion center)
   b) Cortex (gives sights and sounds meaning)
   c) Thalamus (processes sight and sound)
   d) Hippocampus (stored memories)
   e) Spinal Cord (central nervous system)
   f) Hypothalamic-pituitary-adrenal axis (HPA axis)
      (thought and emotion axis)

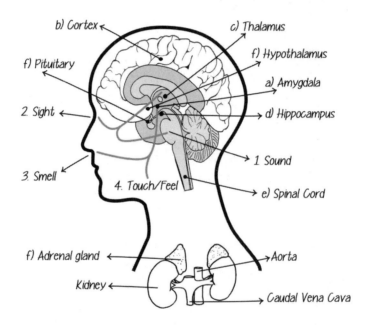

1 Threats that are smell (3) and touch/feel (4) related, are channeled directly to the amygdala (a) which may pass through the Hippocampus (d) and then immediately triggers the fear response which delivers a powerful combination of stress hormones throughout the central nervous system by way of the Spinal Cord (e).

2 Threats that are sight (2) and sound (1) are first channeled through the thalamaus (c) which evaluates size and shape, the information is then passed onto the Cortex (b) which gives the information meaning and then goes to the amygdala (a) which may pass through the Hippocampus (d) and then immediately triggers the fear response which delivers a powerful combination of stress hormones throughout the Central Nervous System by way of the Spinal Cord (e).

3 Thoughts that are threatening or catastrophic are believed to be processed through the hypothalamic-pituitary-adrenal axis (HPA axis) first and then passed onto the amygdala (a) as if the threat were REAL which may pass through the Hippocampus (d) and then immediately triggers the fear response which delivers a powerful combination of stress hormones throughout the central nervous system by way of the Spinal Cord (e).

Anatomy of a Panic Attack

Today, our primary stressors are things like money, feeling overwhelmed, traffic, co-workers' attitudes, body image, keeping up with the Joneses, and more serious crises like divorce, death, and addiction, to name just a few. They may not have teeth or claws, but these types of stressors very clearly threaten our livelihood, our security, and our serenity. And our brains respond to them in the very same way our ancestors' brains did to wolves and bears.

See the problem? Few of today's stressors require us to be able to run faster or fight harder. And because our stressors happen over a longer period of time, we don't have the "sudden" experience that our bodies were designed to respond to. But we still have to survive in today's world, where things feel threatening, though rarely on a physical level. Our bodies and brains have not yet evolved or adapted to help us survive in a modern world with modern stressors. That ancient cocktail of power-packed chemicals keeps getting released, but it's no longer getting used in the way it was intended to be used. We would be better served by our central nervous system if it better regulated the release of these powerful chemicals to cope with fewer life-threatening stressors. We are essentially functioning in a modern world with antiquated equipment.

So what happens when you sit behind your desk, awash with panic that your angry boss will lose his cool and you will lose your job? Or as you lay awake at night, paralyzed by the fear that your wayward teenager will go too far in drug experimentation or addiction and lose her life? Or as you sit in traffic, enmeshed in mental dread that your spouse is having an affair and will leave you? The stress hormones cortisol and adrenaline accumulate in your system, becoming toxic to your brain and your body. Remember, these chemicals were intended to be immediately released from the body through the exertion of running or fighting. If you don't do something to excrete or counterbalance these powerful but potentially toxic hormones, you are going to find yourself very sick. In fact, it has been estimated that as many as 90 percent of all doctor's visits are stress related.[5] Stress is not just a feeling. It's a chemical reaction. Stress has been shown to play a role in heart disease, asthma, obesity, diabetes, migraines, depression, gastrointestinal disease, Alzheimer's disease, accelerated aging, and many more common complaints. And as you can see, unmanaged chronic stress, anxiety, and physical illness go hand in hand.

Now, of course, almost every human being faces stress in the modern world. But not all of us suffer from anxiety disorders or panic attacks. The key, then, is not how much stress we experience—it's how well we cope with it, and how we respond to the inevitable stresses in our lives.

Let's take a simple example. You're driving home from work after a long, tiring day, and someone cuts you off in traffic. You brake to make space for him and avoid a collision. How do you perceive this event? Do you shrug your shoulders and say to yourself, "I guess he must need to get somewhere more urgently than I do." Or do you think, "That jerk nearly ran me off the road! What if I'd had an accident and wasn't able to work? What if I ended up in the hospital? Who would pay the bills then? I'd lose my job . . ." In the first scenario, that stressful moment would just wash over you and you'd move on. But in the second, as you start thinking about all the terrible things that could have happened, you're sending messages to your brain that you're under threat, triggering the release of stress hormones and, in some cases, setting yourself up for a full-blown panic attack. What's the differentiator in these two scenarios? A series of thoughts.

Thoughts Are Chemical

My biggest breakthrough in understanding anxiety was something I heard from Dr. Bernie Siegel. He said: "Thoughts are chemical. They can either kill us or cure us."

Thoughts are chemical. What does that mean? Basically, it means that our thoughts (and our emotions as well, for that matter) have been shown to affect our brain chemistry. Dr. Siegel explains that while doctors and scientists don't yet understand all the specific ways in which brain chemicals are related to emotions and thoughts, an increasing number agree that "our state of mind has an immediate and direct effect on our state of body."[6] What does this mean about anxiety? Well, first it means that anxiety is not just in your head. It's caused by a chemical imbalance in your brain that can be triggered by thoughts and feelings. So while it's not *all* in your head, it may start in your head.

For centuries, there has been an ongoing debate between the worlds of science and psychology as to whether anxiety is biophysical (of the body) or philosophical (of the mind), which raises the question, should it be treated with medicine or psychotherapy? Scott Stossel, in his informative and entertaining book *My Age of Anxiety* (which I highly recommend for anyone seeking to understand anxiety better), gives a meticulously researched history of the debate. "For all the advances brought by the study of neurochemistry and neuroanatomy," he writes, "my own experience suggests that the psychological field remains riven by disputes over what causes anxiety and how to treat it. . . . The clash between cognitive-behavioral therapy and psychopharmacology is merely the latest iteration of a debate that is several millennia old."[7]

What Stossel reveals is that the mind-body debate goes all the way back to the Greeks. For example, Hippocrates, the ancient Greek doctor, concluded that anxiety was a physical problem and believed that "body juices" like bile caused the problem. At the other end of the spectrum, the philosopher Plato was certain that only philosophers could address anxiety, as he believed it was a result of disharmony of the soul. The conflict between the two schools of thought unfortunately still lingers today, although we're making progress. If you consider that "thought is chemical," the logical conclusion would be that there is no separation between the mind and body. Mind is body, and the solution to problems like anxiety is a mind-body treatment.

But I'm jumping ahead a little. Before we get to the solutions, let's dig a little deeper into the causes of an anxiety disorder. What I've explained so far in this chapter is what happens during the actual experience of a panic attack—what's going on in your brain and body during those brief but intense episodes. The next big question we need to understand is, *why?* Why you? And why me? What makes some of us more susceptible to anxiety than others? What makes some of us handle stress just fine, while others find themselves spiraling into panic?

CHAPTER TWO

Anxiety Disorder:
What Causes It and Who's at Risk?

We cannot choose our external circumstances,
but we can always choose how we respond to them.
—Epictetus, *The Enchiridion*

When I began my quest to understand the causes of my condition, the one thing I felt sure about was that I had a family history of mental illness and my number was up. Some people win the lottery; I won a bed in a psych ward. Oh, lucky me! Besides my self-pity over my genetic inheritance, I knew intuitively that something else had to have factored into my breakdown besides genetics, because I had been very well at one time. In fact, despite my life's adversities, I had accomplished more than the average bear.

I didn't have a formal education at that point in my life, yet was earning more money than most with bragging rights to advanced degrees. By my late twenties, I had been General Manager of a company that replaced automotive parts for the insurance business in Dallas, Texas, and had also had the privilege of doing some television and print modeling and acting work. I knew I had a place of high-functioning wellness in me and couldn't imagine that at thirty years old, some gene had just decided to pop up out of nowhere and tackle me to the ground and then take a few pot shots while I was down!

I also knew that I had been under an enormous amount of stress in the preceding months. I had a rambunctious, fearless eight-year-old boy who was adjusting to the loss of one of his eyes from a freak accident on Christmas Day. Leaving my precious baby girl at the sitter's every day after spending every waking moment with her for the first thirteen months of her life was also no small emotional feat. I was plagued with fear for both of them regarding their safety, happiness, and well-being and longed to be with my baby to watch her grow. At the same time, I was also struggling with challenging marital issues which contributed to my anxiety, making my world feel vulnerable and unsure. Add to all that the pressure of my current job as a sales rep, whose income was solely contingent on cold calling every day of the week (which is, by the way, one of the most stressful jobs on earth), and it starts to seem hardly surprising that I was stressed out.

Major Influences on the Development of Anxiety Disorders

This was pretty much the extent of my knowledge and awareness on the day I walked out of that psychiatrist's office and set out on my journey to decode anxiety disorders and finally answer the question: "What happened to me, and *why*?" Quickly, I learned that the answer was much more complex than I could have imagined. Even today, more continues to be revealed about the roots of this condition. As with many forms of mental illness, anxiety does not have a single, clear-cut cause. However, there are several factors that have been identified as playing a role. These include:

- ❧ **Environment.** This refers to many elements of life. For example, how we were raised—were our parents authoritarian or absent? Where we were raised—the climate, conditions, and socioeconomic standards. Were we supported or oppressed by religion? Were we bullied in school? Where we live now. The nature of our relationships and the emotional climate of our homes and work place. The level of satisfaction in our lives. Any traumas we may have experienced in our lives. And so on . . .

- **Genetics.** This means the DNA we were born with, which is much more complicated than it looks at first glance. Genetic traits from many generations back have the ability to emerge seemingly out of nowhere. Geneticists are exploring the possibility of inheriting the effects of generational traumas like genocide and slavery. If there is truth to the idea that these events alter the genetic markers of those who suffered, it doesn't seem too far-fetched that the imprint would be passed on.

- **Personality.** This refers to the individual personalities we are born with and the ones we develop as a result of experiencing life, which are also heavily influenced by how those around us process their experiences.

- **Brain Chemistry.** This refers to each individual's balance or imbalance of neurotransmitters in the brain and their patterns of behavior. For example, many people suffering with anxiety have deficiencies in serotonin, norepinephrine, and dopamine.

- **Chemical Use.** This refers to all of the chemicals we ingest, including foods that have been influenced by modification with hormones, antibiotics, and pesticides. It also includes chemicals like alcohol and drugs, body soaps, shampoos, and essentially anything that can be absorbed through the skin. It includes all chemicals that can and do penetrate our bodies by way of mouth, skin, nose, vein, and muscle.

While all of these factors can play a role, some seem able to influence other factors, and some are more powerful than others. For example, you may have certain genetic predispositions, but your experience of the environment you grow up in is what determines how those genetic traits express themselves. Our environment lays the foundation for how we think about, feel about, process, and perceive our experience of life. And remember, thoughts are chemical. Even our genetics can be altered by learned behaviors and thought processing. The one factor that has the potential to trump all others

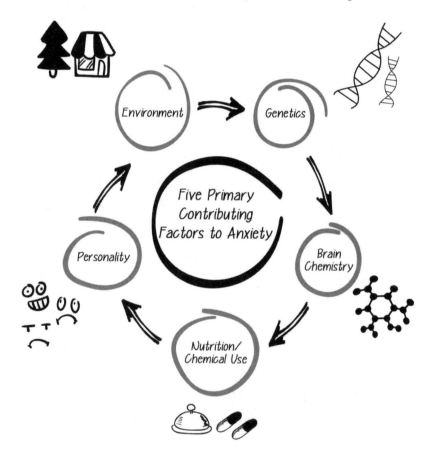

Contributing Factors to Anxiety

is chemical use. You can go to therapy and take your medication until the cows come home, but if you are drinking several cups of coffee a day, for example, you *will* feel anxious. In fact, caffeine is used in clinical trials to cause panic attacks so they can be studied.[8]

At first glance, it appears that the primary factors in the development of anxiety disorders can be attributed to the environment a person grows up in. But when we look closer, this statement does not quite hold up. After all, if you think about it, different people respond completely differently to the very same events.

Have you ever wondered why some people can appear to have so much misfortune in life but seem to be happy and content? Perhaps you are acquainted with someone like the woman behind the counter at the local convenience store who walks to work every day because she can't afford a car, has never been married, and wears the same pair of pants seven days a week. And yet she is the eternal optimist, greeting everyone she encounters with a smile that would light up the Texas sky.

And then there are others who seem to be blessed with every advantage and privilege in life, yet still manage to be miserable—like the successful businessman who pulls up with his beautiful wife in his shiny Mercedes to that same store and steps out in his Armani suit with a scowl on his face to buy a packet of cigarettes. Why the difference? These examples are of opposite ends of the spectrum. Most of us fit in somewhere in the middle, depending on what day it is. But the puzzling question remains: why does one person perceive the world as a wonderful, loving place of discovery and another see the world as a cutthroat, untrustworthy, dangerous place to be endured?

The Power of Perception

If we're trying to understand anxiety, this is a very important question. As discussed in the previous chapter, the difference between a calm, no-problem response and a full-blown panic attack can start with a difference in perception of any given event. It's not about *what* happens to us; it's about *how we perceive it.* And the ways that we perceive the world are shaped throughout our lives by a combination of our life experiences, our genetic predispositions, our personality types, and so on.

Philosophers dating back to Aristotle used to believe that human beings were born as blank slates—*tabula rasa*—upon which life would slowly form personalities, opinions, and so on. I think there is a lot of truth in this theory, although it doesn't take into consideration our inherited psychological genetics. If you've had the pleasure of watching a baby in its first years of development, there's no question that he or she is born with many personality characteristics like temperament, social interest and engagement, curiosity, energy, and determination that cannot be attributed to anything other than genes. Beyond genetics, however, there is absolutely no question that significant events in our lives impact the way we see our world—particularly traumatic events. These shifts in perception, which occur as the result of life-altering events, are what I call new perceptual lenses, because they alter and color the way we see the world. As best-selling author and business consultant Stephen Covey puts it:

> Each of us tends to think we see things as they are, that we are objective. But this is not the case. We see the world, not as it is, but as we are—or, as we are conditioned to see it. When we open our mouths to describe what we see, we in effect describe ourselves, our perceptions, our paradigms.[9]

We see the world not as it is, but as we are. And who we are is shaped by the events that have happened to us and the ways in which we interpreted those events. This is a natural human process—it's how we make meaning out of our world. It only becomes problematic when the meanings we make are based on destructive and untrue messages that we adopted as a result of traumatic events. I call these "thought myths."

As humans we have a natural, instinctual response to trauma, which is to derive a set of beliefs about an event as a protective measure against future trauma. Unfortunately, some of the beliefs cause more harm than good if we have poor coping and processing skills. For example, I had a patient who was an unfortunate victim of an infamous restaurant shooting in New York City that left many people dead and injured. The event was obviously very traumatizing for him, and as a result, he developed a thought myth that all public places were dangerous. He lived the next thirty years of his life experiencing terror in public settings before he was able to get help in processing this event in a more factual way. This example is a more extreme case of an anxiety disorder called Post-Traumatic Stress Disorder (PTSD). Yet the same principles of over-generalization can apply to any traumatic event.

If you're trying to understand an experience like anxiety, you will need to understand the specific traumatic events in your life that made you susceptible to this disorder, and even more importantly, the messages you heard and adopted from those events and the thought myths you created. Remember, the individual lenses that we create as the result of trauma are as personal and individual as we each are. The experience of trauma is relative. One person's trauma is not necessarily the same as another's, even if there may be similar events involved.

Creating a Trauma Time Line

A common technique used to identify pivotal trauma events in the life span is to tell your life story using a trauma time line. To demonstrate how this works, I will first tell you my story and then show you what it looks like in a time line.

I was born in 1962 in Odessa, a small Texas oil town. We were considered middle class in that era, yet looking back it seems like we were hovering just above the poverty line. But we didn't know it. My parents' union began when my father, fresh off a boat after a two-year stint in the Navy, walked into a Sears Roebuck store in a shopping mall with some buddies, spotted a beautiful woman behind the counter, and asked her on a date to win a bet. Eight days later they were married—not exactly ample time to get to know the person you plan to raise a family and spend the rest of your life with. Oh well, they did have good intentions. But I know it won't surprise you though when I say it was a rough ride.

Some of my earliest memories are of the impromptu road trips we took when Mom would walk out on Dad, bundling me, my older brother, and later my younger brother into the car to spend the night at grandma's house or with one of her friends. They eventually divorced when I was in the first grade, followed by a reunion marriage when I was in the third grade, followed by another divorce, followed by a series of remarriages that added up to a grand total of thirteen. That's right, thirteen marriages. Including their two marriages to each other, my mother married six times, my father married seven times. There were nine step-parents and twenty-something step-brothers and sisters. I know it's confusing. I wouldn't believe it myself if I hadn't lived it. Can we say, "no coping skills" all together now!

Perhaps surprisingly, there was no domestic violence between the adults in any of the marriages and little visible fighting, and no other children were born to my mother or father after the original three in our family. There was almost no alcohol present in any of the homes and marriages. However, that hardly meant that these were happy, healthy homes—far from it.

My mother's third marriage, to my first stepfather, was the most destructive for me. At first, he seemed to genuinely care about my mother, my brothers, and me. He was handsome, funny, charismatic, engaging, and it didn't hurt a bit that he had a pasture full of ponies. Real live horses. I thought I was in step-daddy heaven— so much so that I was willing to deny acknowledgment of my own father since, as I reasoned at the time, I now had a better daddy.

Just before my eleventh birthday, and a few short months after the nuptials, my new daddy started paying special attention to me for a specific reason. It turned out he was a pedophile. Sadly, I was not his first stepdaughter victim and there were strong suspicions his own daughter fell prey to his advances as well. I was, however, the first to file legal charges against him for his crime, to which he eventually pled guilty.

Unfortunately, the legal system at that time, in the early seventies, did not know how to protect innocent children from being further traumatized by its insensitivity. As part of the "solution" to avoid facing my offender in court, my attorneys decided it would be a good idea for me to take a polygraph test to prove my claim of being sexually violated. I remember my dad and stepmother taking me to a very large building in downtown Dallas that morning. We walked into a room with three men in suits. One of the men said, "follow me." My parents were not allowed to go with me, and there was no one to reassure me and explain what was going on.

The man in the suit took me into a small room with a two-way mirror, a desk with the polygraph equipment on it, and two chairs. One chair was for me and the other for him. He sat me down and wrapped a strap around my chest that would monitor my breathing, and then he put something on my finger and strapped my wrist to my chair. He told to me that I could only give "yes" or "no" answers to the questions. I was not allowed to ask for clarifications or explain anything in any way.

The process began with simple questions asking me to confirm my name, age, and so on. The machine had multiple needles that scratched the paper with ink from side to side. "Did you have breakfast this morning?" he asked. My heart began to speed. My mind was racing back and forth feverishly, like the scratching needles on the paper, trying to remember if I had had anything to eat that morning. I couldn't remember. But I wasn't allowed to say anything except yes or no. As I sat there, strapped and bound in a chair with my integrity, my truth, my mind, and my soul under the intense scrutiny of the man in the suit and this ominous needle-scratching machine, I had my first panic attack. And it was all recorded. I could hear the needles scratching faster and faster as my heart beat faster and faster. It was devastating.

Somehow, I recovered. I got through the rest of the questions. I passed the test, and my stepfather was convicted of felony child molestation charges with a three-year probation sentence and a three-year sentence to see a psychiatrist. But my life as I knew it was never the same safe place again.

I was certainly fortunate to have had the support of my mother and father throughout this entire ordeal. The night I told my mother what had been happening was the last time I ever saw my stepfather. She never questioned the validity of my story, but immediately took me out of school and moved with me to a friend's house until she was able to get some legal advice. She was advised to place me in the sole custody of my father since her legal marriage to my offender did not offer me protection from his right to be present in her residence.

I promptly moved in to my father's home. My father was in a new marriage to my first stepmother. She was a beautiful, classy woman who was unfortunately insecure and ill-prepared to nurture and support a traumatized stepdaughter. She did the best she could with what she had, I'm sure, although our relationship often left me feeling inadequate—like dirty, damaged goods—and lucky to have a place to live.

It wasn't long before that marriage met its end, and my mother's divorce from the perpetrating husband came through. I was finally able to return home to live with my mom and brothers—just in time for my mother to marry again. Needless to say, I was emotionally devastated by this marriage. I felt a deep sense of betrayal and vulnerability to life and my mother's inability to protect me. I remember, at this moment, making a conscious decision that I would no longer take any advice or direction from either of my parents, as they were clearly far too screwed up themselves to make any productive, protective decisions for me. I had a self-destructive case of justifiable rebellion and was determined to use it to its fullest capacity.

I set out to fulfill my rebellious intent by looking for love in all the wrong places. I sought to find validation as an attractive, valuable, and worthy young woman at the tender age of thirteen through activities usually reserved for the more mature, such as drinking in local bars, staying out till two in the morning, and, of course, having sex. Not surprisingly, by fourteen, I was pregnant with my first baby.

For some reason, I was convinced that I would never see the age of twenty-one, and was sure this would be my very last chance to experience having a child of my own, so I insisted on carrying the baby, even though I knew raising it myself would not be an option. I was far too young, and life at home continued to be tumultuous. My mother's fourth husband had just suffered a devastating brain hemorrhage. He survived, but was left with the mental and physical capacity of a four-year-old. My mother was rapidly slipping into a deep depression and was barely able to cope. Ironically, my teen pregnancy offered me a badly needed reprieve from the reality of my life.

In my second month, I moved into a residential adoption facility for teen minors in Ft. Worth, Texas. My baby girl was born on August 24, 1977, weighing 8 pounds, 5 ounces. I spent a very short ten minutes holding her in my arms on the third day of her life, before I said goodbye forever. As I stepped into my boyfriend's car, I would begin a long journey of accepting my choice to place my beautiful baby girl up for adoption, which, at that time of closed adoption laws, meant I would never see her or attempt to contact her for as long as we both shall live.

In a tragic twist of fate, on that day I was also mourning the devastating loss of my closest friend. While in the hospital, I got a call telling me that my dear friend Karen had been tragically killed in a car accident the day after my baby was born. This loss ran particularly deep for me, because I was carrying an added burden of guilt, having denied Karen's many requests to see and talk to me during my pregnancy. I didn't want her to see me pregnant. I felt that unlike me, Karen was a good girl. I had it all planned that after the birth and adoption of the baby I would pick up my life, and my friendship with her, where it had left off. It was not to be.

Shortly after my return home, my mother's fourth marriage was ending, and she was quickly on her way to marriage number five. Things were actually looking up with this one. Although life was taking its toll on her, my mother was a beautiful woman inside and out. Bruce was a successful public relations manager in the entertainment industry. By this time, I had developed into an attractive young woman in my own right and Bruce noticed—in a healthy way, thank goodness.

He encouraged me to pursue my dream of being an actress and facilitated me signing a contract with a local talent agency. I was always given preferential treatment in any promotions Bruce was doing in his own business that might require a young model/

actress. It was an exciting time, a time when I felt special. But this marriage didn't last either. When my mother's marriage to Bruce ended, I was about seventeen years old. The next marriage that would take place would be my own.

I think you get the picture—and it didn't stop there. What I learned when I was in the psychiatric hospital was how this series of events led me to adopt certain messages about myself and the world, which set me up for my struggles with anxiety.

Based on the stories I just shared with you, the illustration included here demonstrates what my trauma time line looks like. Notice that I have given each event an impact number from 0–10, reflected in the length of the lines I drew. This is the impact that I personally felt, not what I think it should have felt like.

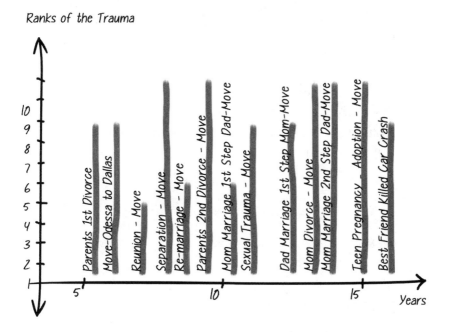

Suzanne's Trauma Time Line

Once I created my time line, I was able to analyze each event by answering four questions:

What were the messages that I heard?

How did I interpret these messages?

Which ones did I adopt as my own?

What behaviors have I developed as a result?

Here's how that looked for the first few events on my time line:

TRAUMA: *Parents' Divorce/Remarriages*

Messages I heard: Marriage is not for forever. Parents' relationship is unpredictable and unreliable, unstable.

How I interpreted the messages: Parents don't care if I'm okay or happy. I can't rely on parents for happiness or stability.

Message I adopted: I can't trust my parents with my happiness.

Behavior as the result of trauma: Hopelessness, depression, and rage.

TRAUMA: *Frequent Moves Due to Marriages/Divorces*

Messages I heard: Where I lived and how nice a place I lived in depended upon whether my mother was with my father or someone else.

How I interpreted the messages: My home environment was contingent on my mother's relationships, which were unstable.

Message I adopted: My environment was unstable. I couldn't trust my mother or father to give me a safe, comfortable, dependable place to live.

Behavior as the result of trauma: Social withdrawal.

TRAUMA: *Sexual Abuse*

Messages I heard: My stepfather's affection for me was a lie. His relationship with my mother was a lie. His promises of a great life were a lie. He threatened my safety and well-being.

How I interpreted the messages: Men's affections are not always what they seem. I can't trust my mother to keep me safe from men.

Message I adopted: Men can't be trusted. Men think I'm pretty and want to touch me. They like that.

Behavior as the result of trauma: Early sexual experimentation, sexual promiscuity

TRAUMA: *Trauma from the Legal System*

Messages I heard: The legal system did not take care of me like I thought it would. I felt like the guilty one.

How I interpreted the messages: Don't trust the legal system.

Message I adopted: I was guilty. Don't trust men in suits in the legal system. Men can't be trusted.

Behavior as the result of trauma: Disrespect of authority.

TRAUMA: *My Own Rebellion*

Messages I heard: My parents don't know what is right for me. Neither do I.

How I interpreted the messages: When I rebel, I pay a price. But I justify it.

Message I adopted: I get hurt when I rebel, but I'm entitled to hurt myself because everyone else does too.

Behavior as the result of trauma: Entitled self-destruction, use of alcohol and drugs.

Sometimes our childhood trauma is obvious, as in the case of my sexual abuse. But other times, it's harder to detect on first glance. Melanie, one of my childhood friends, had what I thought to be a perfect life. Her parents were still married, and they had lived in the same house since she was born. Her family was active in the Church. Yet over time I watched my friend rebel against her family and society. She began to use drugs and alcohol excessively. At seventeen she moved into an apartment with her boyfriend, which was host to round-the-clock drug parties. Her family completely abandoned her and she appeared to feel little impact.

I often reflected on her circumstances, comparing them to my own. I knew why I was messed up! I just couldn't figure out how and why Melanie had gotten so messed up. Her dad even offered to buy her brand new car if she would go to college—a college that he would pay for, of course. I was completely baffled. But what I came to understand was that she experienced a love and acceptance from her parents that was contingent on her fitting into the nice neat little box they had prepared for her. She was not allowed to have her own opinions, path, or personal expression. I'm not just talking about her rebellious behavior as a teen. This pattern of conditional love and acceptance had been present much earlier in her life, eventually leading to her more serious self-destructive and rebellious behavior.

The message Melanie grew up hearing through parental demonstration was: "You are only as good as your willingness to be who we want you to be." Anything less was unacceptable. Ironically, an interesting self-defeating human behavior we tend to adopt in our developmental years is the process of adopting someone else's opinion of us and setting out to prove them right!

Here's how an entry from Melanie's trauma time line might have looked:

TRAUMA: *Abandonment by Parents*

Messages she heard: Love and acceptance by parents is contingent on my perfection.

How she interpreted messages: I will never really have the love of my parents because I'm not perfect.

Message she adopted: I'm imperfect, so I'll act that way because my parents never really loved me anyway.

Behavior as the result of trauma: Drug and alcohol abuse, self-destructive choices.

As a therapist, I have seen hundreds of trauma time lines. Sometimes what is not in the time line is more important than what is. For example, I had one patient, Julia, in her late twenties. She was in treatment for advanced-stage alcoholism, depression, and anxiety disorder. A common theme in Julia's story was the constant verbal abuse she endured from her mother and brother. She was a heavyset young woman and was constantly berated by her family about her weight. They would call her unthinkable names. These abusive messages eventually translated into: "You'll never find anyone who will marry you—you are worthless, stupid, and will never amount to anything." Yet her family's expectations were for her to be a doctor. They even sent her to the most expensive schools in the world for an education in medicine.

The message Julia got was: "You can't, won't, aren't capable of accomplishing anything of worth, but you'd better hang on to the last thread of family belongingness." Her response: failed attempts at school, weight loss, and relationships that led to early-onset advanced alcoholism. Basically she was killing herself with drink.

What was shocking about Julia's time line was that she did not initially include any of this abuse or emotional abandonment by her family. I suspect there were two reasons why. The first was that she had become desensitized to the abuse to the point that it was almost normalized for her as she grew up in that environment. The second was that if she acknowledged it, she would have to do something about it, which for her meant permanently taking herself out of the environment. She was not yet willing to do that.

After working with Julia, I was able to help her create a more truthful time line. Here's a sample entry:

TRAUMA: *Verbal abuse by mother and brother*

Messages she heard: My brother was smarter and better looking. My weight determined my worth and value in the world.

How she interpreted messages: I wasn't as good as my sibling. I was socially unacceptable. My mother loved my brother more me. My brother didn't love me anymore because of my weight.

Messages she adopted: I am no good. I'm not loved or lovable, I am not going to make it in life.

Behavior based on trauma: Failure in academics, attempted suicide with alcohol.

The willingness to be honest with yourself is the most important factor in determining your experience of trauma. Are you ready to find out what happened, how you processed it, what messages you got from your environment, what messages you adopted as your own, and what you did as a result?

EXERCISE: *Create Your Trauma Time Line*

I suggest you fill in your time line privately as you reflect on the significant events in your life. First, find a large sheet of paper or a white-board. Draw a vertical line with the word "birth" at the top and the word "present" at the bottom. Mark your line for each decade of your life (age 10, 20, 30, and so on). And then begin entering the significant trauma events. As you record each one on your time line, draw a horizontal line to reflect the severity of impact on your life from 0 to 10 (see my example on page 33). Write a short description of the trauma above each line.

Once your time line is complete, use your Journal to analyze each event using the four questions below and write down your answers:

What were the messages that I heard?

How did I interpret these messages?

Which ones did I adopt as my own?

What behaviors have I developed as a result?

Afterwards, you may want to tell your story to someone you trust. This is helpful because sometimes we are too close to our own stories to see the obvious. Someone else may offer important insights that you may have missed. However, be careful not to compare your trauma to anyone else's. This is your story and your feelings.

What Are You Afraid of?

As we look back at all the examples of trauma time lines here and your own, we can see that the protective messages we create as a result of our trauma are all fear-based. When I was in Alcoholics Anonymous, recovering from the alcoholism I'd developed through my attempts to self-medicate, I remember them telling us that when you boil it down, there are really only two types of fear: the fear of not getting something we want or need and the fear of losing something we already have. I found this a very powerful way to think about it. Consider your own examples. What are you afraid of losing or not getting? The "something" may not be a thing at all. It may be a feeling, of safety, adoration, attention, respect, encouragement, love, and so forth. And, it may in fact be a "thing," like money, possessions, or property.

Knowing what you're afraid of is critical in determining what new thought-response is appropriate to begin the recovery process from anxiety. For example, if I'm afraid of someone leaving me, I can challenge that fear by acknowledging that if someone leaves me, he or she most likely wasn't a healthy person to have in my life to begin with, and I might be better off in the long run if we were apart. This new thought softens the fear of a traumatic event that hasn't happened, and makes it much less likely to become fodder for obsessive worry in the present.

Now that you've identified the trauma in your life, the fears it created, and the messages and behaviors you created and adopted along the way (which are clearly no longer working for you), you can begin to appreciate why the lenses through which you're seeing the world have become a bit foggy and distorted. And if this is the case, you can appreciate why they may have led you down a path that ultimately wasn't best for your well-being. That's understandable, given the environment you were in at the time. But the good news is that today is a new day, and it's a new time in your life. Today, you get to change those old, worn out, misshapen, foggy, skewed lenses and thought myths for ones that help you see clearly so you can get to where you want to go. You get to choose your path in life. You get to choose how you view the world, the people in your world, your place in your world, and—most importantly—your experience of your world.

CHAPTER THREE

The Surprising Science Behind Neurogenesis Meditative Therapy

What's Thought Got to Do with It?

Make not your thoughts your prison.

—William Shakespeare, *Antony and Cleopatra*

If anxiety is a chemical imbalance in the brain, and thoughts are chemical, then the answer is simple, right? Change your thoughts; change your life. Well, yes. But if you've ever tried to change your thoughts, you'll know that it's not quite as simple as it sounds. "Think more positive thoughts" sounds like a good idea, but that's just like rearranging the furniture in a house with a rotten foundation. To combat an ailment like anxiety, you need to go deeper than that. You need to change thought at a cellular level.

What does that mean—at a cellular level? When a thought enters your brain, certain synapses get activated that transmit information from your neurons to your cells. When thoughts get repeated over and over again, these "neural pathways" become established. This explains the difference between just knowing something as an idea and really knowing it deeply. For example, you might know that you have to move your fingers across a piano keyboard to produce music. But that doesn't mean you know how to do it. A skilled musician has the ability without even thinking about it to sit down at that piano and create beautiful sounds because his or her brain has developed neural pathways that hold this information. Those of us who don't know music in this way don't have these pathways. Can we create them? Yes, with lots of practice. If we are diligent about learning and experiencing music in this way, our brains will eventually begin to develop the pathways to hold this memory information at a cellular level.

This is true for any skill we learn, whether is a physical behavioral skill or a thought behavioral skill. And it's also true for the deep-seated messages we've received and adopted as a result of childhood trauma. The "thought myths" discussed in the previous chapter are patterns of thought that have created deep pathways in the brain. For example, it might make sense to you conceptually that you are a valuable human being and worthy of a safe and loving relationship. But you might not know this at a cellular level. Perhaps your life experience has given you the message that you are a mistake—flawed, scarred, and hopeless—and you have powerful neural pathways communicating this self-destructive information message (which, by the way, are sending a signal to release the stress hormones cortisol and adrenaline because your environment feels threatening to you, based on your self-perception.)

In order to change this, you will need to create new neural pathways through deep contemplation and repetition, much like the process of changing the structure of a muscle. It requires concentrated effort to deliver the new message: "I'm a smart, creative, and loving human being worthy of being loved in the most beautiful way." Sounds like music, doesn't it? Well, just like music, it takes practice and intention. Like the skilled pianist, you need to practice with intense focus until thinking more positively becomes your new natural. Then you will be able to pick up the instrument of your mind and play beautiful uplifting thought-music throughout the day.

So now you understand what you have to do: Change your deeply held thoughts and beliefs, at a cellular level, through practice. But how? When I was in the hospital, I discovered one tool that made more impact than any other when it comes to changing thought. That tool was meditation.

Bringing Meditation Down to Earth

Okay, before I lose you to images of shaven-headed monks and new-age navel-gazing hippies, let me just say that when I was first introduced to meditation back in the psych hospital, I had no preconceived ideas about it. Nothing. And I was so desperate I was willing to try anything. I was one of the most compliant patients in the world (something I would later learn is very rare—patient compliance being one of the biggest barriers to recovery and wellness.) I was sick, I wanted to be well, I didn't know how, and I trusted that my doctors and therapists knew how to help me, so I did everything they told me to do. Happily. Period.

While I didn't have any negative religious influence or ideas about the practice of meditation when my counselor suggested I try it, I know that many people find it a more difficult pill to swallow. ABC News anchor Dan Harris, whose story I mentioned in chapter one, addresses this in his book *10% Happier*: "Meditation suffers from a towering PR problem, largely because its most prominent proponents talk as if they have a perpetual pan flute accompaniment." Harris admits that he himself thought of meditation as "the exclusive province of bearded swamis, unwashed hippies, and fans of John Tesh music," but came to realize that "my preconceptions about meditation were, in fact, misconceptions." In his enlightening and informative book he tells the story of how this happened, and encourages readers to look at this ancient practice afresh. "If you can get past the cultural baggage," he writes, "what you'll find is that meditation is simply exercise for your brain. It's a proven technique for preventing the voice in your head from leading you around by the nose."[10]

Although it has its roots in various religious traditions, dating back as far as 1500 BCE, these days the practice of meditation is also increasingly being used in secular contexts, particularly health-related ones. That's the way I'm presenting it in this book, although if you like to meditate as part of a religious or spiritual practice, that's great too.

Meditation is a difficult word to define, as it is a broad term referring to numerous loosely related practices, and it tends to be used in different ways in different contexts. Generally speaking, meditation usually involves sitting quietly in a state of deep relaxation and focusing the mind—either on one's breath, or on a few words (traditionally known as a *mantra*), or on whatever thoughts and feelings are arising. Meditation can also be done while standing or walking. I like to define meditation as a deeply relaxed state of the conscious mind that allows the unconscious mind to reveal its deepest truths and open itself to new truths.

The National Center for Complementary and Alternative Medicine identifies four elements common to most types of meditation: A quiet location; a specific, comfortable posture; a focus of attention; and an open attitude. This last element is particularly important. They describe it as follows: "Having an open attitude during meditation means letting distractions come and go naturally without judging them. When the attention goes to distracting or wandering thoughts, they are not suppressed; instead, the meditator gently brings attention back to the focus."[11]

I consider myself lucky to have been unburdened by preconceptions, misconceptions, or any other kind of conceptions when it came to meditation. As a consequence, I had no fear and immersed myself completely. The results were astounding. I found a peace I had never known before. For the first time ever, I felt comfortable in my own skin. I liked my own company. My mind became a safe and pleasurable place to be. I noticed that I began to have a new physical response to stressful events. Instead of getting emotionally entangled in something that was someone else's issue, I was able to observe and be compassionate.

So if you're suffering from anxiety, as I was, I'd ask you to put aside any preconceived ideas you may have about meditation, and try it. Try it a few times—remember, it's "exercise for the brain" so you may need to do it repeatedly before you see results. If you're still on the fence, let me explain how it helped me, and what I've since learned about why it was so extraordinarily effective.

The first kind of meditation I tried was guided by one of the therapists. She just told us how to sit, and then instructed us to practice not thinking about anything but our breath. Well, this is nice, I thought. This feels good. I like the way I feel when I'm in a deep state of relaxation. It was hard at first; my mind kept wandering and I'd have to bring it back to my breath. But overall, it was a positive experience. Want to try it? Here's a very simple meditation you can do right now.

EXERCISE: Breathing Meditation

Step 1. Relax into your chair or place of rest.

Step 2. Make sure your body is in an open position where your arms and legs are not crossed.

Step 3. Make sure there are no distracting elements in your environment (such as television, children, etc.)

Step 4. Draw your intention to your breath and notice what it feels like to breathe. Notice the sensation of drawing air into your mouth and throat; feel how it travels down through your body; become aware of how your chest and abdomen rise as it fills your lungs; see how it flows out of your body, and feel the relaxation as your body responds to the release of your breath. As you continue to breathe, contemplate the miraculous nature of breath. Realize that without this involuntary action, there would be no experience of life. Notice how much you tend to take it for granted. Allow yourself to be filled with gratitude for this effortless and essential process.

Step 5. When you are done, slowly count to three and open your eyes.

That's really all there is to meditation, in the most basic sense: that intense focus on one thing. Feeling it physically, noticing it, contemplating it, being with it in the moment, and nothing else.

Meditating with a Script

My first meditation script was given to me by a therapist I was seeing shortly after my hospitalization. Up until this point, I'd simply meditated on my breath in the way I described above. She instructed me to follow the script to help me guide myself into a deep state of relaxation and then meditation. I liked this because it added some pleasant visuals for me to imagine. I really enjoyed seeing the images with my mind's eye. I was able to focus every ounce of my attention on the visuals I was imagining. The script also suggested that once I get into a deep state of relaxation, I repeat three positive words to myself. That then became the entire focus of my meditation, those three positive words. For me, they were usually something like *calm, healing,* and *loving.* I had a meaning attached to each of them. *Calm* was an affirmation that my mind and body were calm. *Healing* was an affirmation that I was getting better every day. *Loving* was an affirmation that I am a loving being worthy of being loved.

The first script I ever used came from Transcendental Meditation (often known as TM), which was in fact the form of meditation practiced by the Beatles and popularized in the sixties and seventies following their much-publicized trip to India. Founded by the Maharishi Mahesh Yogi, this school of meditation aimed to offer people the benefits of meditation without any particular religion affiliation. While TM has struggled to maintain its credibility with science and the Catholic and Christian Churches, today it is growing again in popularity thanks to the efforts of David Lynch and his Quiet Time Program for schools. It is proving to have a profound impact on improving academic scores and reducing stress and violence.[12] I have a deep appreciation for TM, although it is not the particular type of meditation I teach.

Following is a script for a simple five-minute meditation. You may find using a script a little awkward at first until you memorize some of the basic steps, but once you do, you will be able to take your mind on its own journey. I used this type of meditation very effectively for more than a decade. If you prefer to listen to the script aloud, you can visit my website (EscapeAnxiety.com) to download an audio version. You can also have someone read it to you (if you can get through it without laughing!)

If you choose to read the script to yourself, simply read it silently and follow its instructions. I suggest you read it through from beginning to end first and then begin the meditation, following the instructions step by step. Once you have done this kind of meditation a few times, you will find that you can set the script aside and just close your eyes and do the visualizations without needing to refer to it.

When you meditate, it's important to breathe in the right way. The correct way of breathing is important to maximize the relaxation response in the body. Most people breathe from their chest, especially Type A people. This is known as thoracic breathing. The correct way to breathe is by using the diaphragm. When the diaphragm expands through abdominal breathing, all the internal organs are massaged and bathed in fresh oxygenated blood—especially the heart. When our bodies are in a relaxed, open position, and we are using abdominal breathing, they can derive the same benefits as physical exercise by stimulating circulation, thereby increasing the supply of oxygen to our cells.

Don't get discouraged if you initially have a hard time calming your mind. Just simply return your thoughts to your breathing until you can rest your mind. Then return to the script and resume your journey for peace of mind.

FIVE-MINUTE
GUIDED MEDITATION SCRIPT

To prepare for this meditation, find a quiet place without interruption.

Convince yourself that outside noises will not disturb you. Remind yourself that this guided meditation exercise is for your highest good.

Begin by tightening your muscles as tightly as you can. Tighten your face, neck, and shoulders, and hold it. Now, tighten your arms, fingers, legs, and toes. Hold it. Now release—release completely. Allow your body to be limp and relaxed.

Take a moment here and if you choose, invite your spiritual guides, your God, or your angels to join you on this relaxation journey.

Now, take a deep breath into the fullness of your lungs.

And exhale, releasing all of the stress from your mind, body, and spirit.

Breathe in again deeply, the air of confidence and surety.

Breathe out fear and doubt.

Breathe in the air of peace and tranquility.

Breathe out all controlled thought.

Now, being conscious of your mental and physical state of relaxation, on the count of three you will double your relaxed state

One. Two. Three.

You are now walking in a beautiful field of green on a warm spring day. You can feel the moist green grass caressing your feet with each gentle step you take.

Feel the warm sun on your shoulders and a nice soft breeze against your skin and moving through your hair.

You are at complete peace and overcome with a sense of gratitude for the opportunity to be at one with the beauty and the wonder of the earth.

You can hear the trickling of a brook just ahead. You are drawn to the poetic sounds of the playfully flowing waters, moving over, around, and under the smooth polished rocks, large and small.

As you reach the babbling brook, you are awed by the simple beauty of Earth's innocence, unaware of your presence. The brook is a continuous glistening wellspring of calming sounds and mesmerizing images of purity and beauty.

The waters are clean and clear, happily moving down the natural path created by their flow.

As you find a place to sit quietly, reach over and dip your hand into the flowing waters.

Notice that all of your personal fears, anger, jealousy, worry, doubt, and resentments are traveling in the stream toward your hands. Allow them to come into your hands and just let them slip away one by one. Allow them to float through your fingers without resistance, and let them go.

Allow each one of them to float farther and farther away until you can no longer see the last of them. The last one of them is slipping from your sight. Let them go, they are of no good. Each and every one of them is standing in the way of you residing in peace of mind.

Let go of your fears and self-doubt, knowing that your past does not predict your future.

The past is gone, today is a new day.

When you are ready, slowly count to three and you will gently emerge from your meditation feeling relaxed and rejuvenated.

I hope you enjoyed that simple meditation. Don't worry if it felt a little awkward using a script—you will soon get used to it. In part II of this book, as we go through the 8 Steps of the Escape Anxiety process, each chapter will include an NMT meditation script designed for that particular step. It was this type of meditation that began to change my life. It was only later that I would learn that it was changing my brain and my body, too.

As I progressed in my recovery, I was becoming very attuned to the sensations in my body. I was beginning to recognize how different foods made me feel, how my body responded to different environments and people, and how it responded to what I was thinking about. On one occasion, I was relaxing in my tub, which was and always is my favorite place to meditate, and I was in a deep state of meditation. I noticed a light tingling sensation in my head, which obviously was coming from my brain, and then I noticed that I could feel this pleasant sensation traveling down my spine and arms and even my legs. I didn't know what was happening. But intuitively, I sensed that meditation was causing some kind of change in my brain. I realized, at that moment, that meditation was a lot more than just a pleasant experience of relaxation.

The Science of Meditation

It turns out I was right about meditation having an effect on my brain. For millennia, meditation practitioners have intuited this, but now, thanks to breakthroughs in brain imaging technology, science is beginning to be able to demonstrate what's actually going on inside our heads when we meditate. Meditation, once viewed as simply a peaceful and somewhat enjoyable spiritual practice, now finds itself the center of attention as one of the most effective therapeutic interventions for mental health related issues. Even hypnosis is slowly but surely making its way out from behind the veil of suspicion and superstition and gaining some respect from the medical community. This is a remarkable time in history, indeed! Here are just a couple of examples of the fascinating science being done.

Some of the most astounding evidence I've seen of meditation affecting structural change in the brain through the growth of new neurons comes from a 2005 study by Harvard-trained neuroscientist

Sara Lazar and her team at Massachusetts General Hospital. The scientists compared twenty Buddhist Meditators who had been practicing Mindfulness Meditation for an average time of nine years to a control group who were matched in age and demographics but did not meditate. They took MRI scans of the brains of participants and found significant differences in the amount of gray matter in the frontal cortex among those who meditated. They summarize:

> Brain regions associated with attention, interoception and sensory processing were thicker in meditation participants than matched controls, including the prefrontal cortex and right anterior insula. Between-group differences in prefrontal cortical thickness were most pronounced in older participants, suggesting that meditation might offset age-related cortical thinning. Finally, the thickness of two regions correlated with meditation experience. These data provide the first structural evidence for experience-dependent cortical plasticity associated with meditation practice.[13]

The study sample was small, but nevertheless presents compelling evidence that meditation may cause the aging process in two very important regions in the brain to be slowed down by up to two decades. These are the areas related to sustained attention and concentration functions, interoceptive attention (internal body awareness), and emotional control.

A more recent study, by researchers at Wake Forest Baptist Medical Center, entitled "Neural Correlates of Mindfulness Meditation-Related Anxiety Relief" (June 2013), sought to identify brain regions activated by mindfulness meditation and their impact on anxiety symptoms. Summing up the evidence they found in a *Psychology Today* article, Christopher Bergland writes:

> Brain imaging found that meditation-related anxiety relief was associated with activation of the anterior cingulate cortex, ventromedial prefrontal cortex, and anterior insula.

These areas of the brain are involved with executive function and the control of worrying. Meditation-related activation of these three regions was directly linked to anxiety relief.

Activation of the anterior cingulate cortex—the area that governs thinking and emotion—is the primary region believed to influence a decrease in anxiety. These findings provide evidence that mindfulness meditation attenuates anxiety through mechanisms involved in the regulation of self-referential thought processes.[14]

This is just a small sampling of the fascinating meditation studies that are available to us today. When I began teaching people how to meditate, I would always share a little bit about the science behind what we were doing. I can't tell you how many times I would hear, particularly from the men in my groups, things like "this is first time I ever understood why it's important to meditate," or "I always thought it was a bunch of woo-woo." Anytime I can help someone become a believer in the restorative power of meditation, I know I have done a good day's work. Knowledge truly is power.

Creating an Escape Route

My own practice of meditation grew organically following my hospital stay, and I added other methodologies I had learned, such as a simple relaxation technique involving tightening and relaxing the muscles and various images to engage all the senses from the mind's eye. I also began to add altruistic messages like compassion for others and messages of encouragement and inspiration to reframe old worn-out belief systems.

In an effort to make sure that what worked for me would also work for others, I began to volunteer at Brighton Hospital, a leading dual-diagnosis hospital in Brighton, Michigan. I went each Sunday evening and taught meditation to patients who wanted to participate. At the time, I called the classes Spiritual Fitness. Back then I struggled to clearly describe what I was doing in the meditations. Nevertheless, they loved it! It helped them to get some measure of relief from their mental anguish. I knew I had a gift that many would be able to use and benefit from.

I also began to study with the legendary Dr. Anna Spencer who founded the Medical and Dental Hypnotherapy Association. This is where I discovered the capacity we have for learning and integrating new information during a state of deep relaxation and/or meditation; which is essentially the same thing as hypnosis. Yes, hypnosis. Again, I'd ask you to set aside your preconceptions about this term—I'm not talking about magic tricks or mind-control. Hypnotherapy is a powerful clinical tool, as I'll describe in more detail later in this chapter.

I integrated what I'd learned into my meditation work, and created the first version of the Escape Anxiety program, which I began to use as a clinical intervention with patients suffering from anxiety. The patients loved it and found great relief, hope, and direction as a result. They were truly finding the program to be an "escape route" from the agony of anxiety. Yet I was still struggling to define exactly what it was. What I was doing wasn't really just meditation; it also wasn't really just guided imagery. It wasn't just hypnosis either. It was a little of all those things with the added element of thought reframing, which is central to the treatment known as Cognitive Behavioral Therapy. What I was doing didn't fit neatly into the box of any theory that existed.

Eventually, I chose the term "Neurogenesis Meditative Therapy" to define the unique style of integrated meditative therapy I had developed. Neurogenesis simply means the new growth of information messengers in the brain. Meditative Therapy means using uninterrupted, focused attention to affect positive change. This name felt like a fit to me because the most important message I wanted to impart is that this therapy works at the cellular level. These therapies cause a chemical change in the brain, much like antidepressants do.

They help you create more serotonin and dopamine excretions—naturally. So you might be asking then, why isn't everyone doing this instead of taking medications? Good question.

Meditation vs. Medication: Which Is Best for You?

The short answer to the question I just raised is this: most of us are instant-gratification people. We are of the opinion that it wouldn't make sense to wait thirty days to feel better when we can take a pill and feel better today. And remember, the pharmacological treatment for anxiety predated an official acknowledgment of anxiety as a disorder in the health professionals' diagnostic manual, which naturally gave precedence to pharmacological treatment. Let's also remember the centuries-old standoff, for lack of a better term, between medical science and psychology. Fortunately, with the kinds of studies I've cited in this chapter, we are at the beginning stages of merging the two sciences and recognizing that there is no separation between mind and body. However, there's a long way to go.

Most therapists who support alternative or holistic approaches like Neurogenesis Meditative Therapy stand firm on one their side of this line, advocating psychological treatments for anxiety and firmly opposing psychopharmacology. I am not of that mindset. I believe there is no separation between the mind and body. Therefore, I think the treatment of anxiety should always include psychotherapy because the most prevalent problem is within the thought, reason, and perception part of the functioning mind.

But that doesn't mean pharmacological treatment might not also be an appropriate intervention to regulate chemicals in the brain related to physiological disorders Whether pharmacological treatment is advised should have everything to do with the patient's needs rather than the treatment professionals' biased views. One thing I do feel strongly about is that pharmacological intervention should never be prescribed to the exclusion of psychotherapy. And I can't imagine a reputable prescribing physician who would not agree with this.

The pharmacology industry has unfortunately created a double-edged sword with the introduction of the benzodiazepines class of drugs, which include Ativan, Xanax, Valium, and Klonopin, to name a few. One the one hand, they are the most effective drugs on the market to offer an almost immediate relief from the symptoms of anxiety. On the other hand, they have an unfortunate anxiety-inducing rebound effect upon withdrawal. These drugs have highly addictive characteristics and are intended for short-term interventions only. They are also associated with a 50 percent increase risk in dementia.[15] In 2005 there were a staggering fifty-three million prescriptions filled for Ativan and Xanax. That number continues to rise. Chemical dependency centers are seeing an alarming number of patients with long-term addictions to these powerful drugs and the dangerous combining of them with alcohol and other street drugs.

Non-narcotic psychotropic medications, particularly the class of drugs known as serotonin-norepinephrine reuptake inhibitors (SNRIs), have been found to be highly effective in treating anxiety for most people. They do, however, take time to work and most people have to spend a considerable amount of time trying different ones to find out which one works best since there is not currently an exact science to guide them. Hopefully one day physicians will be able to analyze blood samples to determine prescription and dosage. Unfortunately we are not there yet. Because of this, if you feel you may need pharmacological treatment, I recommend finding a prescribing physician who is willing to listen to you and pay attention to your responses to the medication and spend the time trying several medications to find the right one.

One thing I hope to impress upon you is that the brain—for all its mysterious and wonderful powers—is just another organ. It is just as vulnerable to illness or dysfunction as the liver or the heart.

It's unfortunate that many people, myself included at one point, seem to believe the brain should be immune to illness and therefore shouldn't require medication. We are embarrassed to need medication for regulating the chemical imbalances in our brains. This error in thought has contributed to much long-term suffering from mental illness. When I was first prescribed medication, I was relieved because I felt better. But when my doctor told me I might have to be on medication for the remainder of my life, I wasn't relieved at all! I was offended. How dare he think I might need to take psychiatric medications for the rest of my life? I felt fine. Okay, I may have felt fine because I was on the medication. But still—it bothered me.

He explained it to me this way: "If you had come to me with diabetes and I told you that you would have to take insulin for the rest of your life to be well, you wouldn't have a problem with that would you?" I said, "No. But . . ." "But there is no difference," he replied. "Your brain doesn't produce the right balance of chemicals for you to be well without some help from medication." I couldn't deny that it made perfect sense, even though I did feel disappointed.

What I also came to understand is that just like most illnesses, if mental illnesses are caught early enough, they are more easily treated with brief interventions. But if they are caught at a later stage, they may require long-term treatment including medications, as in my case. This is why is it so important for our culture to begin using the kind of coping skills I'm sharing in this book as preventative medicine rather than response medicine. I can tell you with 100 percent certainty that my mental illness would have never reached the stage of requiring hospitalization if I had had the benefit of the information, tools, and coping skills I am offering to you now. But if your condition has progressed to a point where non-medicinal interventions are not enough, that's okay. There is no shame in taking medication for your brain, just as there is no shame in taking medication for your heart.

Five Methods Used in
Neurogenesis Meditative Therapy (NMT)

Let's take a closer look at the different therapies that I've integrated into this program. In the history of psychology, as well as philosophy, the advancement and addition of new theories and practices goes through an evolution process of its own. As awareness, learning, and measurement of efficacy increase over time, new theories and practices emerge from professionals in the field.

Most of these new practices take parts of old practices and add new things to them, building upon what has come before while improving and refining it. Neurogenesis Meditative Therapy is no exception. The NMT guided meditations in this book bring together in a new and powerful way five meditative and therapeutic interventions that have been found to be the most effective treatments for stress and anxiety related disorders. Let's examine these five modalities first, so that you will be familiar with the techniques I will be inviting you to try and the reasons they are effective and powerful. They are:

1. Progressive Relaxation

2. Mindfulness Meditation

3. Guided Imagery Meditation

4. Hypnosis and Hypnotherapy

5. Cognitive Behavioral Therapy

Progressive Relaxation

Herbert Benson, MD, founder of the Mind/Body Medical Institute and Associate Professor of Medicine at Harvard Medical School, coined the term Relaxation Response. He defines it as "a physical state of deep rest that changes the physical and emotional responses to stress"[16] and emphasizes that it is the opposite of the fight or flight response. One of the most effective ways to induce this response is to use the process of Progressive Relaxation, which is a technique developed by Dr. Edmund Jacobson in the 1930s. Quite simply, it involves tightening and relaxing your muscles, with awareness, in a methodical way. I use this as an effective means to deepen the mind and body into a state of relaxation in preparation for the meditative therapies. You'll see a version of this process near the beginning of each of the meditation scripts in this book.

Mindfulness Meditation

Mindfulness is the most simple of all the meditation practices. Originating in the Buddhist tradition, it has recently become widespread in secular contexts as a means of stress-reduction. Mindfulness is not about finding a deeper level of spiritual awareness or trying to empty the mind of thought. It's simply the practice of being in the now. Right here, right now. Not in the past, not in the future, but in the present. You simply narrow your focus to what you are experiencing right in this moment. For example, what does it feel like to breathe right now? What do the clothes you are wearing feel like against your skin? What are the sounds you are hearing in the room or outside the window? What does your stomach feel like right now, or your back, or your feet? What smells do you smell? If your thoughts are getting away from you and you are beginning to feel the physical sensations of anxiety, this practice can be powerfully grounding.

Jon Kabat-Zinn, founder of the Mindfulness-Based Stress Reduction program at the University of Massachusetts Medical Center, writes "Mindfulness means paying attention in a particular way: On purpose, in the present moment, and nonjudgmentally."[17] These days, thanks to the efforts of Kabat-Zinn and others, mindfulness is being widely used to alleviate a variety of mental and physical conditions. Due to the simplicity of this practice and the absence of religious affiliation, it is more easily adaptable to all walks of life and thus is being implemented in psychiatric and chemical dependency treatments centers worldwide, as well as in businesses, schools, prisons, and many other settings.

Guided Imagery Meditation

One of the foremost leaders in the practice, development, and research of Guided Imagery is Belleruth Naprastek. She defines Guided Imagery as "a gentle but powerful technique that focuses and directs the imagination."[18] It involves the creation of images that engage all the senses. The employment of symbols and metaphors during the process of meditation is what separates this practice from other types of meditation. Guided Imagery, Naprastek writes, "has the built-in capacity to deliver multiple layers of complex, encoded messages by way of simple symbols and metaphors."[19] I believe it's a more gentle approach because the messages are implied rather than direct. The efficacy of Guided Imagery has been impressively substantiated by a large body of research conducted by many Universities as well as the armed forces. It has been shown to be effective in reducing side effects from cancer treatment, reducing fear and anxiety prior to surgery, managing stress, and managing headaches.[20]

Hypnosis and Hypnotherapy

Okay, let's talk a bit more about hypnosis. I intuitively knew that hypnosis and meditation had some similarities, but I was confused by the entertainment side of hypnosis. I knew the practice of hypnosis on a therapeutic level was very effective. People were using it in dental surgeries, childbirth, and even bodily surgeries for those who wanted to avoid going under sedation for medical or other reasons. They were also using it to quit smoking, become better golfers, and overcome the fear of public speaking. So why, and more importantly how, was it being used to manipulate people into doing silly things on stage? Even before I understood what was happening here, it made me a little sad. Here was a serious and effective option for people who were suffering or looking to self-improve, and yet its credibility was being diminished by the media and entertainment industry. So I took a course to become a certified Hypnotherapist in order to find out the truth about hypnosis.

Simply put, hypnosis is a trance-like state of heightened focus and concentration, together with deep relaxation. The American Society of Clinical Hypnosis describes hypnosis as: "a state of inner absorption, concentration and focused attention. It is like using a magnifying glass to focus the rays of the sun and make them more powerful. Similarly, when our minds are concentrated and focused, we are able to use our minds more powerfully. Because hypnosis allows people to use more of their potential, learning self-hypnosis is the ultimate act of self-control." They also add "Recent research supports the view that hypnotic communication and suggestions effectively changes aspects of the person's physiological and neuro-logical functions."[21]

One of the most important things to know about hypnosis is that all hypnosis is in fact self-hypnosis. The idea that it is a form of "mind control" that someone else can impose on you is a myth. For it to work, you have to agree to it. Also, a person will never do or believe anything that is outside their value system under the state of hypnosis. Yes, even the people that are on stage acting like a quacking duck. They are aware of what they are doing and are able to stop at any time they feel it necessary.

Hypnosis, like meditation, has been used since the beginning of time, long before it was called hypnosis. In fact, we do it every-day. Daydreaming is a form of hypnosis. However, in the eighteenth century, Western society was introduced to what we now know as hypnosis. German Physician Franz Mesmer developed an unfortunate reputation for attempting "mind control" but has also been credited for the first awareness of the scientific relevance of hypnosis. Mesmer, whose name gave rise to the alternative term "mesmerism," was also the first to develop a process of induction and used his natural charisma and flair for the dramatic to incorporate costumes and mystical figures. Unfortunately his magical twist on this important psychological therapy led to his exile from the scientific community.

By that time, however, there was no denying that hypnosis worked. By the nineteenth century, medical professionals like John Elliotson and James Esdaille, convinced of its medical impact on the healing process, went so far as to risk their reputations to use it with their patients, and researchers like James Braid shed light on the physical aspects of the state. Thanks to these efforts, hypnosis was finally accepted as a clinically sound intervention to aid in the healing process and has since been applied in the great universities and hospitals of our time.

What we understand today about the power of hypnosis is that being in a deeply relaxed state of being, we naturally "let our guard down," suspending our critical mind. Remember the perceptual lenses, talked about earlier, that we create from trauma? In a state of hypnosis or deep relaxation, these bias lenses relax so that new information can reach our subconscious mind. This allows new information to more effectively become a knowing experience (like the example of the skilled musician) rather than just an understanding or intellectual experience. This is why hypnosis is so very effective in changing thought, perspectives, and behavior.

So, what is the different between hypnosis and meditation? Meditation is passive; hypnosis is directive. This is why it is very important that you trust the person who is guiding your hypnosis session. You are in a very vulnerable, highly suggestible state of being. This is why stage hypnosis works and can be fun and entertaining. But more importantly, it works beautifully for the purpose of psychological healing by effecting thought and behavior change.

Take a look at the diagram illustrating how hypnosis works to better understand the concept.

Conscious Mind
Logic, reasoning, analyzing, decision making, will power & working memory

Critical Mind
This is the filter between the conscious and subconscious mind. It is the information gatekeeper of what goes into the subconscious mind.

+ −
Scripts

Subconscious Mind
This is the source of our deeply embedded positive and negative ideas, habits, that form the ways we impulsively respond to the world around us, based on our recessed memories of trauma, pain, joy, and achievement.

Hypnosis works by reaching beyond the Critical Mind to inform the subconscious mind of new, more helpful ways of thinking and behaving.

How Hypnosis Works

Cognitive Behavioral Therapy

Cognitive Behavioral Therapy was developed through an integration of behavior therapy with cognitive psychology research in the 1970s. CBT is most commonly an interactive treatment between therapist and patient in which the patient is guided to examine the relationships between thoughts, feelings, and behaviors. One of the objectives of CBT is to identify patterns of thinking and core beliefs that lead to self-destructive behaviors. This type of self-discovery enables the patient to develop more effective thought patterns to improve coping. The National Alliance for Mental Illness states that, "Scientific studies of CBT have demonstrated its usefulness for a wide variety of mental illnesses including mood disorders, anxiety disorders, personality disorders, eating disorders, substance abuse disorders, sleep disorders, and psychotic disorders. Studies have shown that CBT actually changes brain activity in people with mental illnesses who receive this treatment, suggesting that the brain is actually improving its functioning as a result of engaging in this form of therapy."[22]

Preparing for the Escape Anxiety Journey

When you understand the elements that make up Neurogenesis Meditative Therapy, and are comfortable that they are well researched and effective, you are ready to begin the 8-Step Escape Anxiety Process. Each chapter in part II of this book will guide you through one of the eight steps that I have identified as being essential to master in your quest for freedom from anxiety. These chapters are designed to be both educational and practical, and they include:

- Information about specific beliefs and behaviors that contribute to anxiety

- Stories and examples to illustrate the problems you're tackling

- ❧ Quizzes that you can complete to assess the severity of your anxiety

- ❧ Exercises that will help you understand and manage your symptoms

- ❧ A NMT guided meditation script to help you integrate and absorb what you have learned in each step

Work through these chapters at your own pace, giving yourself the time you need to understand and process the information and complete the exercises and meditations. If you find yourself struggling with any particular step, I encourage you to stay with it and repeat the exercises and meditations until you feel confident you have absorbed the ideas and practices.

In preparation for your journey, I suggest you choose a journal or notebook that you can use to complete the exercises and also to track your progress. You may also wish to dedicate a place in your home for the meditation practices—somewhere you can be comfortable, peaceful, and uninterrupted.

Are you ready to embark on your escape route out of anxiety and into emotional freedom and peace of mind? Then let's go . . .

Part II

8 STEPS TO FREEDOM:
THE ESCAPE ANXIETY PROGRAM

CHAPTER FOUR

Step 1:
Conquering Codependent Control Issues

Selfishness is not living as one wishes to live,
it is asking others to live as one wishes to live.

—Oscar Wilde, *The Soul of Man Under Socialism* (1895)

A key common denominator for those who suffer anxiety, unbridled fear, and panic attacks is an intense need to control. The first step in the Escape Anxiety program is getting your control issues under control!

We all have control issues, to some extent or another. We develop control issues because our world feels out of control. Our attempts to control others become a problem when the relational discord we create as a result of our need to control becomes more painful than the feelings of a lack of control we were seeking relief from in the first place. Now, it must be said that people who are "controlling" are well-meaning people. What it boils down to is the fear factor.

Remember how we talked about the two kinds of fear in chapter two? Fear-based anxious thoughts are at the root of control issues. We feel a need to control people, places, and things because we're afraid we might lose something we already have or not get something we want/need. For example, we're afraid other people won't do something as efficiently as we can and we'll lose time. We're afraid other people will make a mistake and it will reflect poorly on us, putting our image, reputation, social standing, job, or relationships at risk. Control issues can take any number of forms that in the end boil down to fear.

We also feel the need to take on the responsibility of the world because it is clear to us that the world is not taking responsibility for itself. We are extreme caretakers and rescuers extraordinaire! We put on our directors' hats, and with megaphone in hand, proceed to direct everyone else's life. Sometimes, when we realize our controlling behavior is no longer working and our actors and stagehands are going on strike, we throw off our directors' hats and sink into the abyss of anxiety, isolation, depression, hopelessness, and even suicidal fantasies. We don't know what to do next when people will not do, think, act, feel, not feel, say, or believe what we need them to. And besides, we are convinced we know what is best for everyone! Why won't they just listen and fall in line? By this time, anxiety is raging out of control.

Whether you are attempting to exert unreasonable control over others or retreating internally in response to feeling that the world is out of control, one thing is for certain: Your peace of mind is dependent on someone else. This is all too common. We care so much about what other people are doing or saying, or not doing or not saying (for their own good, by the way), that we forget about caring for ourselves. Sure, we may look good on the outside, but the constant preoccupation with others has left us in an emotional state of complete self-abandonment.

It turns out there's a psychological term for this, which you may have heard: codependency. Melanie Beatty, author of *Codependent No More*, offers the following definition: "a codependent person is one who has let another person's behavior affect him or her, and who is obsessed with controlling that person's behavior"[23] (By the way, if I had a dime for every time I said "*Codependent No More* is the best book I've ever read on relationships" I'd be a wealthy woman!) In the treatment world, the term "codependent" is most often reserved for the loved ones of an alcoholic or addict, but the truth is, anyone can suffer the emotional and eventually physical ailments associated with the fear-based characteristic of needing to control others. I titled this chapter "Codependent Control Issues" to reflect this fact, and I will be drawing on much of the valuable research that has been done on codependency, as it is equally applicable to the anxiety sufferer.

The reality is that the only person you have control over is yourself, and even in that there are limitations. If you don't place a healthy value on your individual self, and you don't have a clear sense of where your emotions end and others' begin, you are headed for emotional turbulence in the form of anxiety and potentially many other physical ailments.

The Development of the Need to Control

As we develop from early childhood, we begin taking social cues from our environment on how to manage life, with the primary objective being to avoid stress, tension, pain, and anxiety. Many times when we grow up in environments that are out of control, we feel the need to step into a role of control in order to create a sense of manageability for ourselves. This, of course, can happen at any stage of life, but most often these patterns begin to emerge in early childhood.

Control issues can manifest either externally or internally. If we express our control issues externally, we become the directors of the show. We get really good at telling other people what to do, when to do it, and how to do it in order to make ourselves feel better. But sometimes, if we find we cannot control our external environment, we turn our need to control inward. For example, if you grew up in a home where everything had to run smoothly for fear of mom or dad raging out of control, you might develop what's called an internal measure of control. Examples of internal measures of control are stifling or "stuffing" feelings and emotions; types of behavioral control like repetitive actions, such as counting or cleaning, which are commonly related to Obsessive Compulsive Disorder; or eating disorders like anorexia or bulimia. Sometimes we manage internal measures of control by self-medicating. It is all too easy to stuff those emotions with a little alcoholic beverage, pill, or smoke.

These are just a few examples of how unhealthy control issues can develop. There are many more scenarios that can get this ball rolling. Once again, however, we can see how one or both of the two kinds of fear are at the root of our controlling behaviors.

Again, it is important to know what it is that you're afraid of so you can begin dismantling the fear-based thought myths that precipitated the extreme control issues that are making you sick with anxiety.

Misplaced Expectations

One of the key emotional behavioral traits of anxious controllers is the tendency to put all of our happiness eggs in someone else's basket—meaning, my happiness is contingent on your happiness. If you're not happy, I'm not happy. Likewise, if you're happy, I'm happy. We lack emotional autonomy or independence. You're probably familiar with the quote "Happiness is an inside job"? Well, it is, but it's inside *you*, not inside someone else. Yet too many of us make our happiness contingent on others.

Think for a moment about what that means. Our happiness is pretty darn precious. Isn't that what we all strive for in life, above all else? Isn't it more valuable than any tangible item or achievement? Then why would we expect someone else to walk around day and night with all of our happiness eggs in their flimsy little basket and value them as much as we do? No one in his or her right mind would expect something so silly. Well, in fact, many of us do. It's okay, you're not alone.

When we do this, we find that our happiness becomes dependent on key people in our lives behaving the way we want them to. We have to check in to see how they are feeling and what they are doing in order to decide how we are feeling. I've heard it said this way: "I have to take your temperature to see how I'm feeling." We set ourselves up for severe disappointment when our happiness is attached to an expectation we place on others. The more unrealistic the expectation, the harder that basket of eggs falls. This is especially true if we have done something for the other person and have an expectation of something in return. How could they not do what we expect of them? What are they thinking? It's simply the right thing to do. Don't they know that? Here, we have advanced to the martyrdom stage of control.

So the question is, how is this working for us? How many times does the show come off the way we want it to? How many times do people say, "Oh you're right, I'm going to do it that way from now on!" And then actually do it? Almost never, right? Can we really expect people to do what we want them to do when we want them to do it? Even when it makes perfect sense? No, not very often. When our happiness, contentment, motivation, hope, and joy are dependent to our expectations of someone else, we are in for a rude awakening! People change. People get sick. People die even when they think they're not going to. People make bad choices even when they are good people. People are on their own journeys. Of course, it's natural for us to feel disappointments, sadness, and even grief when other people make choices that hurt themselves. But we should be cautious about investing our emotional well-being in someone else's choices.

Control issues can be tricky, just like food issues, because we do need to have some measure of control in our lives, just as we do need to eat. We can't eliminate the issue altogether in order to recover from the unmanageable parts. So where and how do we draw the line for ourselves? The key here is balance and picking your battles. It helps to honor someone else's journey and their right to makes mistakes just like we did. It helps to acknowledge that we have different values and views in life than other people, even when they are related to us. It helps to ask if we may offer our opinion rather than impose it. It helps to visualize standing in the middle of a hula-hoop and accepting that the only person, place, or situation you have control over is in that hula-hoop.

EXERCISE: Who's Holding Your Happiness Eggs?

To gain some clarity on how you may be struggling with control issues, consider the following questions. You may want to write your answers in your journal.

1. Write down the times that someone has disappointed you. What did you lose? What was that you didn't get that you wanted?

2. Write down the names of the people in your life who are holding your precious happiness eggs.

3. Write down the names of the people in your life who you desperately wish would do things differently in their own lives.

4. Now, try to identify what your fears are: What are you afraid of losing and/or what are you afraid of not getting? (Remember these don't have to be "things"; they can be simply feelings, opinions of others, and so on.)

Unveiling the fear-driven motivation behind the impulse to control allows us an opportunity to face and dismantle those fears and begin the process of recovering from codependency.

The Dangers of Codependency

As a therapist I've been witness to some pretty extreme cases of people desperately attempting to control uncontrollable situations and other people. I had a patient who was engaging in sexual behavior that went completely against her value system in an attempt to keep her boyfriend's interest and engagement in the relationship. The first thing she wanted to know about her treatment was when we were going to tell him to stop expecting her to engage in these sexual acts. This is not only having poor boundaries; this is control via people-pleasing to the extent of complete self-abandonment.

For a time, I worked exclusively with the families of the alcoholics and addicts. I heard some examples of desperate attempts to save lives through dangerous attempts to control others' choices— for instance, a grandma who regularly went into drug-infested, gun-wielding neighborhoods to pull her grandson out in a desperate attempt to save him from his addiction. She became so ill, physically and mentally, from her obsession with saving this young man that she had to be hospitalized.

Another example was a mother who attempted to cover up her son's car accident while he was driving under the influence of alcohol by helping him to leave the scene of the accident. She drove to meet him and had him drive his car home in front of her while she followed along to make sure nothing else happened on the way home. She was completely blind to the fact that she had already enabled his hit and run, not to mention the fact that he was also still drunk and her following behind him was in no way whatsoever going to prevent him from having another accident. The only things she did were to prevent him from having to face the consequences of his actions and to put herself at risk of becoming an accessory to a crime.

These examples are extreme cases when the need to control someone else's desires and behaviors led to thoughts and feelings that go beyond normal kinds of self-sacrifice or caretaking. For example, parenting always requires a certain amount of self-sacrifice, and sometimes controlling one's children is very appropriate. However, a parent could become codependent towards his or her own children if the parental sacrifice started to take on unhealthy or destructive forms like those I've just described.

Other common characteristics of persons with controlling behavior include:

- Low self-esteem

- Obsession

- Poor communication

- Raging anger

- Denial

- Sex problems

- Poor boundaries

- Excessive caretaking

The Change Process

Regardless of what you might think about Dr. Phil, he has one thing right. He knows that "we can't change what we don't acknowledge." Awareness of our dysfunctional behavior, well-intentioned as it may be, is our first step in the change process.

The second essential step in the change process is acceptance. I don't mean that you need to accept or make excuses for someone else's unacceptable behavior. I'm suggesting that you accept, in this moment, that it is what it is. I'm suggesting that you work towards accepting your limited ability to change other people, places, things, and situations. I'm suggesting that you accept the fact that other people have a right to their own opinions, paths, and certainly their own mistakes.

Many years ago, I was going through a painful time with my daughter in relation to her self-destructive choices. A friend asked me, "What was the catalyst for the most growth in your life?" I thought for a moment, and then replied, "Pain." She said, "Then why would you want to deny your daughter her own pain?" Oh, what a zinger! She had me. Truth, right between the eyes.

So just as my friend did for me, I'm suggesting that you take off your director's hat and find a chair that just has your name on it. A nice, big, fluffy, comfortable, relaxing chair. Take a load off—it's your time, you deserve it. Acceptance is surrender. When we accept our powerlessness over one aspect of our lives—for example, other people—it allows for more power over another part of our lives, such as ourselves. When one door closes, another one opens. We haven't lost when we surrender; we have chosen a new direction.

I'm a very visual person, so I have a vivid memory of the point at which I surrendered my director's hat. For me, it was actually a captain's hat. I visualized myself standing at the helm of a huge ship, desperately trying to navigate through a raging storm in violent waters with all my strength. Suddenly, a clear but inaudible message was spoken to me: "Sit down—the ship will reach its destination, in its own time and at its own pace. You can sit down and relax."

I saw myself, depleted from my efforts to control the ship, walk over to the side of the deck, take off my captain's hat, and sit down. The clouds began to clear, the rain stopped, the ship rocked ever so gently. I was just a passenger on a journey. I was not God. I finally surrendered my control. In that moment, I was free. It is true that I often find myself getting back up and struggling to grab that helm. But I am learning, and I know that managing my tendency to attempt to control my life by controlling others is a process of recovery, not a single event.

QUIZ: Do You Suffer from Codependent Control Issues?

Take this simple quiz to find out if your anxiety may be related to codependent control issues. Answer Yes or No to the following questions, as honestly and truthfully as possible:

1. Do you say "yes" too often to help other people and end up neglecting yourself?

2. Do you lose sleep worrying about the choices other people are making?

3. Do you often take responsibility for the actions of another person?

4. Do you work long hours without compensation?

5. Do you show up early for work and stay late because you think your boss needs you?

6. Do you stay late at the office to clean up after your employees or co-workers?

7. Do you obsessively clean the house, do laundry, cook, to please someone else?

8. Do you worry constantly about your kids, spouse, or significant other?

9. Do you take on the child-rearing responsibility for other people's children?

10. Do you have intimate relationships with people who are addicts or alcoholics?

11. Do you find yourself making excuses for other people for their addiction?

12. Do you mask the fact that your family may have been dysfunctional?

13. Do you easily get depressed, fatigued, or sick after helping another person?

14. Do you sometimes feel that mental or physical abuse by another is your fault?

15. Are you taking tranquilizers or sedatives?

16. Do you have a stress-related medical diagnosis?

17. Do you sometimes wish both you and another person were dead?

18. Do you have thoughts of suicide?

Answering yes to three or more of these questions may indicate a problem with codependency.

PLEASE NOTE: *This test is not intended to diagnose; it is a tool to increase your awareness of codependent tendencies. If your life is in crisis because you love someone who is an alcoholic, addict, mentally ill, suffers from an eating disorder, is a sex addict or a gambling addict, please seek the help of a group like Al-Anon or NAMI (National Alliance for Mental Illness) that offers a family-to-family educational and support program to manage your life in the midst of your loved one's crisis. Other helpful resources are Celebrate Recovery (a Christian-based recovery program) and CODA (Co-dependents Anonymous).*

EXERCISE: *Know Your "Cans"*

One of the essential keys in the first step of the Escape Anxiety program is learning the difference between what we can and can't control. Even the most educated and self-actualized of us gets confused about these issues. To decipher one from the other, it is important to write them down, thereby reducing mental clutter. Of equal importance, we must take responsibility for our misguided choices and attempts to control others. Peace of mind is our singleness of purpose for regaining control over our lives.

The good news is, the better we become at accepting our powerlessness over other people's words and actions (or lack thereof), the better we become at controlling our own words (both internal and external) and actions. The result is regaining control over our lives. Now, if that's not motivation to move forward, then I don't know what is!

Take an honest look at a situation or relationship you want to control that is contributing to your anxiety and fears. Then fill in the blanks in each column below. The effectiveness of this exercise is achieved by your willingness to be fearlessly honest. You will find infinite wisdom in this exercise—just apply the principles any time you are struggling with something or someone, and are having the impulse to exert control.

To help you complete the exercise, consider the following example: Someone at work said something about you that was untrue and it made you angry. What can you control and what can you not control?

You can't control the words of another person.

You can't control how she feels about you (she is coming from her own life experience).

You can't control how many people she tells.

You can't control another person's reactions to what she says about you.

However,

You can control what you say and how you act.

You can control how much time and mental space you give to the situation and the woman.

You can make amends if you need to.

You can attempt to correct her perception of you, or the situation, with pure motive, and a pure heart so that you don't make matters worse for yourself.

You can choose to be angry and mentally plot revenge, or you can let it go through forgiveness, and trust that others will see through what she is saying and recognize that you are a good person with no ill motives. (Refer to chapter six for help with this.)

Now, if she was right about what she had said about you, then you would have an entirely different list, wouldn't you? That is, if you are honest.

Notice how all the things you cannot control are about her, and all the things you can control are about you. Yep, that's how it works—it's that easy. Ready to try with a real example from your own life? Again, be fearlessly honest with yourself and think your options all the way through. This is your Escape route from the mental bondage of anxiety, unbridled fear, stress, and panic attacks. How quickly you make your way out depends on your dedication to the process. Believe me when I say it works if you work at it!

Can NOT Control	CAN Control

Take a good look at the items in your *Can NOT* Control column. Hopefully, you have identified what you cannot control. Begin practicing letting it go. Don't give the items in your *Can NOT Control* column any more mental energy. It's useless. It's an illusion. Let it go. Accept the things you cannot change. Otherwise, you will be spinning your mental wheels. This is the place where anxiety and panic breed, gain their power and ultimately dominate your life.

Give all of your mental energy and attention to that which you can control. This is where you are powerful, effective, and truly in control. In turn, this is where confidence, self-esteem, and peace of mind are formed and can gain their power to dominate your life. You have powerful, positive choices to make.

GUIDED MEDITATION FOR CONQUERING CONTROL ISSUES

This meditation builds on the short script we used in chapter three. You may remember some of the visualizations. Allow this script to guide you into an effortless release of your need to control.

To prepare for this meditation, find a quiet place without interruption.

Convince yourself that outside noises will not disturb you. Remind yourself that this guided meditation exercise is for your highest good.

Begin by tightening your muscles as tightly as you can. Tighten your face, neck, and shoulders, and hold it. Now, tighten your arms, fingers, legs, and toes. Hold it. Now release—release completely. Allow your body to be limp and relaxed.

Take a moment here and if you choose, invite your spiritual guides, your God, or your angels to join you on this relaxation journey.

Now, take a deep breath into the fullness of your lungs.

And exhale, releasing all of the stress from your mind, body, and spirit.

Breath in again deeply, the air of confidence and surety.

Breathe out fear and doubt.

Breathe in the air of peace and tranquility.

Breathe out all controlled thought.

Now, being conscious of your mental and physical state of relaxation, on the count of three you will double your relaxed state

One. Two. Three.

You are now walking in a beautiful field of green on a warm spring day. You can feel the moist green grass caressing your feet with each gentle step you take.

Feel the warm sun on your shoulders and a nice soft breeze against your skin and moving through your hair.

You are at complete peace and overcome with a sense of gratitude for the opportunity to be at one with the beauty and the wonder of the earth.

You can hear the trickling of a brook just ahead. You are drawn to the poetic sounds of the playfully flowing waters, moving over, around, and under the smooth polished rocks, large and small.

As you reach the babbling brook, you are awed by the simple beauty of Earth's innocence, unaware of your presence. The brook is a continuous glistening wellspring of calming sounds and mesmerizing images of purity and beauty.

The waters are clean and clear, happily moving down the natural path created by their flow.

As you find a place to sit quietly, reach over and dip your hand into the flowing waters.

Notice that all of your personal fears, anger, jealousy, worry, doubt, and resentments are traveling in the stream toward your hands. Allow them to come into your hands and just let them slip away one by one. Allow them to float through your fingers without resistance, and let them go.

Allow each one of them to float farther and farther away until you can no longer see the last of them. The last one of them is slipping from your sight. Let them go, they are of no good. Each and every one of them is standing in the way of you residing in peace of mind.

Let go of your fears and self-doubt, knowing that your past does not predict your future.

The past is gone, today is a new day.

Make these words your own words:

I am and I have everything I need today.

The impulse to control another human being is rooted in false pride, driven by fear.

I am at ease with the world, myself, and my fellow human beings.

I will not use another human being as my sole source of feeling okay, loved, and accepted.

I will fill my emotional and spiritual cup today by giving all that I desire to receive.

I will let go of my fear-driven old ideas of self-gratification and the satisfactions of getting what I think I need at the expense of another human being.

I will honor other human beings today by accepting their right to their own individual expression of the human mind-body-spirit creation.

I cannot find my peace of mind in your spirit.

I will look within for my own emotional satisfaction.

I cannot find love for myself through your heart.

Love for myself, love for my fellow human beings, love of my god, comes from me. It is in me, it is of me, I am love, loving, and beloved.

Love is Peace. Joy and harmony are my divine, natural inheritances—I claim them, own them, and live in them and through them.

I am wise, intelligent, capable, and able. I enjoy my own company.

Reflection on my life affirms that my emotional, spiritual fullness comes as the result of my own accomplishments, achievements, created by my own creativity, wisdom, love, and grace.

I am in the natural flow of life.

I can change my mind and change my life by living in giving rather than getting.

I will practice forgiveness, grace, and acceptance.

I am of pure mind and good intentions.

I can look into the eyes of another's soul with awe and wonderment.

I will honor their ideas and opinions that have taken shaped and were formed from their own life experience.

I will honor other people today by being understanding rather than having to be understood.

I will no longer have a need to control.

I am in acceptance of my powerlessness of over people, places, and things.

I am free to see what needs to be changed in me.

I am worthy of all that is good.

I will claim my inheritance of love, joy, peace, and harmony.

I am love, joy, peace, and harmony.

I am a beautiful expression of mind-body-spirit human creation.

When you are ready you may emerge from your relaxed state feeling better than you did before, knowing that you are richer in mind, body, and spirit for having had this experience. And so you are.

CHAPTER FIVE

Step 2: Dismantling Perfectionism

The thing that is really hard, and really amazing, is giving up on being perfect and beginning the work of becoming yourself.

—Anna Quindlen
Commencement speech at Mount Holyoke College (1999)

Perfectionism is a characteristic often shared by very successful people. It's also common to anxiety sufferers. Many anxiety sufferers are extreme perfectionists, setting themselves up for a constant experience of failing or falling short. This intense need to strive for success is driven by that now all-too-familiar four-letter word *fear*. Fear of not getting something we want and/or need or fear of losing something we already have. In this instance, the types of "things" we fear losing or seek desperately to hold onto are things like acceptance, respect, adoration, and adulation.

Of course, there's nothing wrong with striving for success. The problem starts when striving for success crosses the line into a stress-induced cycle of unrealistic expectations and self-abuse. These unrealistic expectations set us up for the inevitable pattern of shortfalls that put us on the self-destructive merry-go-round of mental obsession and internal emotional and verbal abuse. That might qualify as a foundation for an anxiety attack, don't you think? Indeed, it does. The personality characteristic of perfectionism is clearly one of the primary contributors to anxiety, and so the second step in our Escape Anxiety program is dismantling these perfectionistic tendencies.

Researcher and author Brené Brown, who has written several books about perfectionism, describes it as "a self destructive and addictive belief system that fuels this primary thought: If I look perfect, and do everything perfectly, I can avoid or minimize the painful feelings of shame, judgment, and blame."[24] She makes a clear distinction between the healthy, positive drive for self-improvement and the "20-ton shield" of perfectionism that in fact holds us down. "Understanding the difference between healthy striving and perfectionism is critical to laying down the shield and picking up your life," she writes. "Research shows that perfectionism hampers success. In fact, it's often the path to depression, anxiety, addiction, and life paralysis."[25]

As Brown points out, researchers have found that perfectionism correlates with depression, anxiety, eating disorders, and other mental health problems.[26] Similar to control issues, it is a coping skill that begins developing in early childhood and eventually becomes self-harming.

Perfectionism usually begins developing quite simply. A child does something good; the parent or caretaker responds with positive attention, which translates to acceptance and the affirmation that he or she will care for the child. The child naturally desires to experience this again, from a very primal need for survival, and so begins the process of striving to get the attention and response from others that makes her feel good and safe. Equally, on a more complex level, perfectionism can be a learned behavior through observation of others' successes and a desire to get what they got.

Unlike Brown, many researchers argue that perfectionism can be a healthy human drive toward self-improvement, and some psychologists have suggested that perfectionism should be subdivided into two types: adaptive (functional for survival) and maladaptive (in conflict with survival). Fair enough. I'm sure you know a perfectionist who is extremely successful as a result of his or her inner drive to improve. But if you suffer from anxiety, chances are your perfection-ism falls into the maladaptive category, so for the purposes of this book, we'll keep our focus there.

QUIZ: Are You a Perfectionist?

If you're not sure to what degree you may have a perfection-ist tendency, ask yourself the following questions:

1. Do you find yourself procrastinating because you get so worried about doing something perfectly that you have a hard time getting started?

2. Have you ever tried something new that you'd like to be good at, but when you found you were not imme-diately as good as you thought you might be, you abandoned it altogether rather than appreciating your progress?

3. When you look at your work, are you able to notice how good it is and feel a sense of accomplishment, or do you only notice the imperfections and worry about what more could have been done to improve it?

4. When you look at others' work, do you notice their imperfections rather than focusing on the high points?

5. When you look at your appearance, do you focus on all the things you'd like to change about yourself rather than noticing what you like about yourself? Or do you simply not think too much about it either way?

6. Do people tell you that you're difficult to please and often negative?

7. When someone gives you feedback and it's 95 percent positive, do you focus on the 5 percent that was just kind constructive criticism or suggestions for improvement?

8. When you are in the process of achieving a goal, are you able to enjoy the journey or do you focus on the end result?

If we were able to identify yourself in four or more of the above questions, it is likely your tendencies toward perfectionism are interfering with your quality of life, peace of mind and contributing to your anxiety. Later in this chapter I will share with you a variety of skills to shift into a more adaptive state of mind and behavior.

Three Faces of Perfectionism

In an article titled "The Many Faces of Perfection" published in the American Psychological Association's *Monitor On Psychology*, Etienne Benson reports that researchers Paul Hewitt and Gordon Flett have developed a multidimensional perfectionism scale that identifies three varieties of perfectionism: self-oriented, other-oriented, and socially prescribed. I find this a useful distinction, so let's unpack what each of these categories could mean.

Self-oriented perfectionism is a self-imposed internal motivation or desire to be perfect. Self-oriented perfectionism is hazardous because it can lead to a toxic loop of obsessiveness, inefficiency, procrastination, and ultimately giving up and giving in. The behaviors that tend to follow these emotional characteristics include poor attendance, poor performance, and low morale.

The self-oriented perfectionist begins the process of obsessing on how to make herself conform to her own self-identified box of perfection, which then leads to inefficiency due to the unattainable high standards that she sets for herself, which naturally leads to being overwhelmed, which deepens the cycle into procrastination, and which ultimately leads to throwing in the towel. Another characteristic common to this cycle is martyrdom. The martyr often believes that she is "the only who cares," "the only one who works hard enough," and "the one who does everything to keep everyone afloat." This conflict is rooted the self-oriented perfectionist's mistrust in others caused by her fears and insecurities, which inevitably prevents open, honest communication. This self-destructive toxic cycle unfortunately not only leads to fractures in relationships; it can also lead to many types of mental illness including anxiety disorders, depression, and obsessive-compulsive behaviors.

One of my patients, Ann, fell into this unfortunate trap of mental illness through her obsession with attaining an unattainable goal. Her story is interesting because she did, at one time in her life, attain the unthinkable. Looking for employment, she had answered an ad in the newspaper for someone with computer marketing experience. It was by all appearances a fairly average job with average pay for someone familiar with computer marketing skills. However, this average job quickly became anything but average. She was doing such a good job, and her boss's business was growing at such a phenomenal rate, that he decided to give her a percentage of this online business. Within just a couple of years, they sold the business and her small percentage netted her several million dollars.

Her perfectionism began to be harmful for her when she found herself jobless, wealthy, and bored. She had imposed upon herself the expectation that she should have a repeat performance of that success. You and I can see clearly that her previous success was partly due to an extraordinarily unusual situation. The odds of that being repeated were comparable to getting struck by lightning twice at the very same spot! Unfortunately, she could not see this, and within a very short period of time found herself isolated, anxiety ridden, and literally drinking herself to death over the self-imposed pain of her perceived failure to repeat her extraordinary success.

Other-oriented perfectionism is a tendency to have extraordinarily high expectations of other people—to expect one's family, co-workers, or friends to be perfect. You can see how this orientation would obstruct the development of a healthy, balanced relationship with others. This may be the most destructive type of perfectionism in terms of social functionality because of the difficulties that arise from having a lack of empathy and an inability to forgive others for their shortcomings. Partners of other-oriented perfectionists fear being honest about who they are and what their true feelings and thoughts are for fear of being a disappointment. The rigidity of this orientation makes those who fall into this category difficult to work with and to build relationships with.

When it comes to a work environment where team-building is needed, this kind of perfectionism can be particularly problematic. It allows no room for a natural flow of messy collaboration, which is what a business partnership often originates from. Because other-oriented perfectionists tend to be uncomfortable with both giving and receiving support and encouragement, it makes it difficult or near impossible to create an emotionally safe and productive environment.

I encountered an extreme example of other-oriented perfectionism in a former patient of mine. This gentleman, Richard, had a very successful virtual events management company that he was able to run primarily from his home. He had built this business from the ground up and was pulling in millions of dollars every year, offering a product he had created that would benefit professionals seeking to make highly technical presentations, virtually. But despite his financial success, he was suffering with debilitating anxiety and was self-medicating, primarily with food, but also with prescription pain medications.

Things were made worse by the fact that he was unable to hire other people to help him manage his enormous business, due to a mistrust in others' ability to perform as well as he thought he could. Added to this was an inability to keep his employees happy because of his constant micromanaging. As a result, he found himself isolated, overwhelmed, near death, and buried in an endless, unmanageable cycle of demands that he couldn't manage. He often referred to his business as "a prison of my own making." All of this arose from his need for others to be perfect and his need to fulfill the martyr role he had unconsciously created for himself.

In this man's process of recovery he was challenged to completely change his perspective on his expectations of himself and other people. Even though for a time his perfectionism had served him well as he grew his business, ultimately it became his gravedigger, until he was able to surrender and seek help. Here you can see that pain pills and food were not his primary problems. These were just symptoms of his anxiety, fueled by his perfectionism. Unfortunately, he wasn't ready to see this. Today he is still struggling to find that perfect person to run his business so he can take enough time off to treat his eating disorder.

Socially prescribed perfectionism is a self-imposed belief that others will value one only if one is perfect. The socially prescribed perfectionist feels as if he is buckling under the constant weight of the perceived unrealistic expectations of others. He can hardly begin to show his imperfections for fear of banishment from society. How can he ask for help when he believes that his lack of knowledge would be interpreted as a sign of weakness or incompetence, which would threaten his ability to belong?

Many men suffer with this type of perfectionism because of socially prescribed gender expectations, although our society as a whole is making progress in changing this gender-specific role expectation. Unfortunately, when there is a shift of this magnitude it is society's nature to swing to the far opposite of the proverbial pendulum before it finds its natural balance, hopefully somewhere in the middle. Rarely do the extremes of these perfectionistic tendencies happen intentionally. They typically arise slowly over time and don't show up on the radar until they become a problem.

The Great Divide

These perfectionist orientations can often lead to what is known in psychology as cognitive dissonance. Cognitive dissonance is an experience of mental anguish or conflict that arises when we're simultaneously holding on to beliefs or attitudes that contradict each other. In this case, the anguish is particularly acute because those contradictory beliefs relate directly to the self.

Here's how it works: All human beings have an "ideal self." This is an inner picture of how you would like others to see you. It is your "best self," whatever that may mean to you. Perhaps it includes your best character traits—such as humor, love of family, or loyalty and commitment—which you would like others to see and acknowledge. However, human beings also have an "actual self." This is how we actually behave. For example, your ideal self might be witty and entertaining, but your actual self could tend to fumble your jokes or choose ones that are inappropriate, leading to unfavorable comments. This would give rise to some pretty painful feelings of failure and rejection.

Or perhaps your ideal self is loving to your family, while your actual self draws negative attention from your co-workers because of your impatience on the phone with your spouse. Again, this would bring up feelings of shame and sadness from disappointment in yourself. Or perhaps your ideal self is confident and capable, yet when you have to speak in a business meeting, your actual self turns red and has a trembling voice, an experience that is only made worse by your embarrassment and self-disgust.

Experiences of cognitive dissonance like those described above occur when the ideal self doesn't match the actual self. This gap between ideal and real is a great divide for many of us, particularly those with perfectionistic tendencies—a yawning chasm into which our self-esteem and confidence tumble, time and time again.

I'll share with you a painful memory of one such instance in my life. My perfectionism tended to fall into the socially prescribed category. I was convinced that other people wouldn't like me, respect me, or do business with me if I appeared anything less than perfect. At the time of my anxiety crash, I was working as a commercial sales rep for the *Auto Trader* magazines. Each day, I had a route on which I would visit different kinds of dealerships—automotive, big trucks, boats, and RVs. All of my income was straight

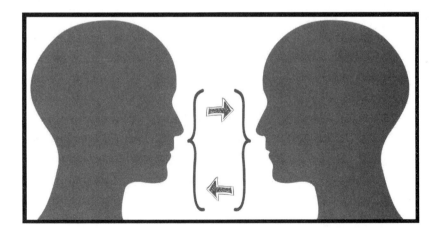

The farther apart our Actual Self gets from our Ideal Self based on our BEHAVIOR, the more mental anguish we experience.

Ideal self/actual self

commission, so I needed to get the most out of each dealership I visited. We made a commission on the individual ads, but we made more money on the nice full-page, full-color display ads. However, making a sale on the big money ads meant going into the big man's office and making a compelling pitch as to why he needed to spend this money with me every week.

On this particular day, I wasn't feeling well. I was already noticing that I was having more and more panic attacks in my customers' offices. I dreaded them like the plague. Each time I had one, I shed another layer of self-esteem. I sank into the vortex of mental and emotional pain that came from doing something so shameful that I couldn't bear to even be in my own skin. I began to fear I would embarrass myself beyond repair by screaming and running out of a car dealer's office like some kind of crazy person. That's what I felt like: a crazy person with a nice, tidy, attractive, well-put-together mask!

Anyway, I was invited to go into the big boss's office. It felt like walking into Donald Trump's office for the pitch of my life! I was all dressed for success—a sharp suit, perfect makeup and hair, and high heels. He didn't invite me to sit, which meant I had about thirty seconds or less to make a sale. I needed this sale. I knew that this sale would offer me some badly needed financial relief, and, besides, it would help me compete with my nemesis, Linda, who always seem to knock the sales figures out of the park.

I opened my mouth, and out came a breathless, quivering, scared, needy, desperate attempt at a throw-me-a-bone I'm-starving wannabe sales pitch. Ugh! My ideal self, a successful, articulate, confident, attractive saleswoman of the eighties was tumbling off the cliff, pushed by my actual self, a panic-attacking, fear-ridden, incompetent-looking sales chick! Although today, I have great empathy for that young woman that I was, I can still recall that excruciating moment as if it were yesterday. No, I didn't run out. I turned, red-faced, sweaty, lip quivering, and gently and graciously walked out of that enormous intimidating office without the sale.

The ugly truth is that if you have a few of these experiences in close proximately to one another, the kind of mental anguish and brutal internal self-abuse that follows such an incident can quickly lead to a mental health crisis, as it did with me.

Unfortunately, this type of pain is often a trigger to the cycle of self-medicating. The easiest and most attainable way for many to ease this pain, at least temporarily, is with a drink, a pill, or a hit off of a joint. It certainly was in my case. The truth is, it worked for me for many years. I could come home and quiet my anxious, pain-riddled mind with a tall glass of wine or whiskey and the anguish would begin to subside. For me and so many others, however, at some point not only was there not enough alcohol to ease the pain, but the alcohol began to prove that it wasn't my friend. The alcohol began to turn on me, and in fact became the cause of more mental anguish because of the behavior I would exhibit under it's influence—behavior that only widened the gap between my ideal self and my actual self.

To some extent, it is natural that we present an image or a "mask" to the world. Back in primitive societies, survival often depended on having some value to the community. When your value was hard to prove or you were competing with someone else's value, you would develop the skill of masking as a survival strategy. The same thing goes on today, as men and women choose their clothing, makeup, hairstyles, cars, homes, and education with one well-rooted primal instinct in mind: *How will people perceive my value in my community so I will be accepted and not rejected?*

This instinct originated in the mating, hunting, spiritual, and cultural rituals of our ancient ancestors. You can even see that many types of insects and creatures have evolved with masked features for the purpose of survival. So it is natural for us to mask to some degree. The common theme, again, is balance and authenticity. This simplest way to explain this is: Do my insides match my outsides? Do I feel as beautiful on the inside as I do on the outside? If I don't, then I will start to experience cognitive dissonance. For example, most people who knew me back in my panic-stricken sales days would remark that I had a calming presence about me, yet if they had known the internal workings of my mind they would have seen a committee of hamsters in a cage, frantically running in circles. This disconnect only added to my anxiety.

Tips for Managing Perfectionism

Here are some more shifts in perception you can use to help you pare down your perfectionism and make your life manageable.

- Set realistic, reachable goals

- Focus on your successes, even partial ones

- Stop zeroing in on your own or others' faults and flaws

- Realize that accomplishments alone do not determine self-worth

- Think about the process, not just the results

- Realize that anxiety and depression are signs that your goals are unrealistic

- Welcome your mistakes; they are opportunities to learn

A good touchstone that can help ensure that your goals are realistic, not perfectionistic, is what is commonly called the S.M.A.R.T. Goal. Make sure your goals are:

- Sensible

- Manageable

☙Attainable

☙Reachable

☙Timely

Perfectly Imperfect

Still hung up on an idea of perfection? Okay, let's pretend for a moment that you could achieve it. Imagine that you are perfect. You live in a perfect little house, with a perfect little family, with a perfect little figure, and a perfect little job. How perfectly boring would that be? If you were perfect, you wouldn't have any needs. You wouldn't need people, comfort, community, guidance, mentors, teachers. Think of all the people in your life who taught you valuable life lessons. They were able to teach you those lessons because they too once needed to learn them. If you were perfect, you wouldn't see the value in anyone but yourself. Think about the people in your life that you appreciate and hold in high esteem, whose friendship and companionship you treasure. How perfectly lonely would life be without them?

When I was in the hospital, I finally had an awakening about perfectionism. I realized that if I were perfect, I wouldn't need anybody or anything. I wouldn't value what I had or be awed by simple pleasures. I wouldn't experience the satisfactions of achievements, growth, learning, and winning. I wouldn't need anyone, and I certainly wouldn't need God. In fact, if I were perfect, I might as well be God, right? All-knowing, all-loving, all-creative, all-powerful—perfect. This was when it dawned on me that God actually intended for me to not be perfect. He made me exactly, perfectly the way I am—perfectly imperfect. Why? So I could need all the beautiful things in life, and experience all the incredible emotions they bring. In a new and powerful way, I realized that there is a God and I am not him or her. I am free to be me. Hallelujah!

This realization set me free in the most profound way. Suddenly, it became perfectly okay to be imperfect; that's what I was supposed to be all along. Embracing my own imperfections was a painful lesson, but well worth the struggle. And, once you awaken to your imperfect self, you never have to learn that lesson again.

EXERCISE: *Know Your "Cans"*

For this exercise, you'll notice we're using a similar chart to the one used in chapter four. This time, one column has the header "Can NOT Change" and the other is headed "CAN Change." Think about the characteristics that you tend to beat yourself up about that you actually cannot change, and write them in the first column. Then, in the second column, list some things about yourself that you would like to change and you know would be possible.

By the way, there are always things about each of us that we have the power to change if we are willing. So remember to be honest. Making excuses not to change is not the same as cannot change. If you aren't willing yet, that's okay, but these items still need to go in your CAN Change column. Check through all the items in your lists to find truth.

I'll give you an example so you can get started. Let's say you hate the way you look. Your hair looks like a rat's nest, you're tired, and you're bulging out of your clothes. You cannot change the physical characteristics you were born with (without surgery). But, here are some things you can change:

✿ You can change your sleep habits to feel more rested.

✿ You can change your attitude about yourself.

☙ You can change your hairstyle or color (men, this includes you, too).

☙ You can change your outfit to better complement your figure.

☙ You can change your eating and exercise habits so, in time, you won't bulge.

Get the idea? Try it for yourself in the chart below.

Can NOT Control	CAN Control

Now, take a good look at your "Can NOT Change" column and practice letting go—with love. If you cannot change it, it is useless to obsess over it. Again, this is where anxiety, fear, hopelessness, and desperation breed and gain power over our lives. Use your power of choice to focus your energy and mental imagery on the things in your life that you can change. Remind yourself that your life experience is a direct reflection of the contents of your thoughts. Contemplate what you are thinking about. You are creating your life experience through your thoughts.

Now look at your "CAN Change" column. Decide which items you are ready to change. For example, to continue with my scenario, maybe you are ready to change your thought patterns but not your eating habits. That is okay. All good things come in time. In order for you to channel your energy into positive mental choices, you will need to temporarily let go of what you aren't yet ready to change, for the moment. Don't spend any more time beating yourself up about habits that you are not willing to change. It's your choice.

Once you have made the decision to let go of the things you cannot change, and put aside the things you are not yet willing to change, you will find the mental energy to focus on the things you can change. You will have less anxiety about yourself and a clearer understanding of how you can use your thoughts to improve your well-being. You will find yourself more able to accept your own imperfections and those of others. This is where you can begin to find peace in an imperfect world.

GUIDED MEDITATION FOR DISMANTLING PERFECTIONISM

This meditation is designed for the purpose of supporting you in loving yourself as the perfectly imperfect creature you were intended to be.

To prepare for this meditation, find a quiet place without interruption.

Convince yourself that outside noises will not disturb you. Remind yourself that this guided meditation exercise is for your highest good.

Begin by tightening your muscles as tightly as you can. Tighten your face, neck, and shoulders, and hold it. Now tighten your arms, fingers, legs, and toes. Hold it. Now release—release completely. Allow your body to be limp and relaxed.

Take a moment here and if you choose, invite your spiritual guides, your God, or your angels to join you on this relaxation journey.

Now, take a deep breath into the fullness of your lungs.

And exhale, releasing all of the stress from your mind, body, and spirit.

Breathe in again deeply, the air of confidence and surety.

Breathe out fear and doubt.

Breathe in the air of peace and tranquility.

Breathe out all controlled thought.

Now, being conscious of your mental and physical state of relaxation, on the count of three you will double your relaxed state.

One. Two. Three.

You are now walking through a safe and peaceful field on a warm spring day toward a beautiful pond.

You can feel the soft, moist green grass beneath your feet.

Feel the warmth of the sun on your shoulders and your face.

You can hear the rustle of the leaves on the trees, and feel the gentle breeze moving through your hair.

As you approach the pond, find a perfect place to sit by the water's edge.

Notice that beside you is a soft, round pebble.

Reach for it and effortlessly toss it into the water.

Notice the ripples in the water from the entrance of the pebble. They grow in size and number then begin to disappear into the edges of the pond.

Now look beneath the water. Your pebble is reaching the sandy floor of the pond. As the pebble comes to rest, millions of tiny sand particles ascend in unison and then each and every one of them begins to descend, encircling and finally resting alongside your pebble.

As your pebble is at rest, so too are you at rest.

When you are irritable, anxious, restless, and discontent with yourself, it is because there is something about yourself that you find unacceptable and unworthy of being loved by yourself and others.

You can shift your perception of yourself and alter your experience of living with and through yourself.

Make these words your own words:

My body is my physical transportation and vehicle of communication for my journey on earth as a human being.

I am my own individual expression of the mind-body-spirit human creation.

I am a spiritual being having a human experience.

I can be grateful for my physical attributes and abilities.

I can be grateful for the window of my eyes through which I view my world.

I can be grateful for my emotional capacity to feel love and joy.

I can be grateful for my mind as my creative, intellectual limitless force.

I am grateful for the miraculous mystery of my life-sustaining organs that work with tireless precision, absent any conscious effort of my own.

My mind, body, and spirit are indeed the most miraculous creation on earth.

My gratitude for my body is my applause to my creator.

My smile, though not perfect, is a perfect reflection of the light of my heart.

My eyes, though not perfect, are perfect windows to the spirit of my soul.

My words, though not flawless, are a flawless representation of contents of my mind.

I am of God, not God.

I am a miraculous creation designed imperfectly with perfect intent.

Perfection leaves no room for wanting, desire, or drive.

Perfection closes the door on compassion and empathy.

Perfection denies the opportunity for community.

Perfection is a divine characteristic, not a human characteristic.

Progress is achievable, perfection is an illusion.

Today I will acknowledge my progress, appreciate my desires, my compassion, and my empathetic heart.

Today I will savor the companionship I find in other imperfect human beings.

Today I will focus on my haves rather than my have-nots and dwell in the house of gratitude.

My body is not the sum total of who I am, though I am immensely grateful for the miraculous, physical creation that I am.

Coming face to face with my own defects of character and shortcomings presents me with choices— life altering, life shaping, life sustaining choices.

When I fall short of the glory of my own expectations, will I hang my head in shame, or will I wrap my arms around my own heart and whisper words of grace and unconditional love?

Will I forgive myself for my own inequities or will I remind myself of my wisdom and strength?

Will I find the courage to try again or will I retreat in fear and miss my opportunity to participate in the wonderful, exciting, unpredictable journey of life?

Will I choose to be subdued by life's obstacles and oppressed by life's challenges or will I greet my day with excited anticipation of the continual unfolding of a panoramic life?

When I am tired and weary from the sharp curves and tight corners of my life's travels, will I suppress, tame, and cage the fearless adventurer within or will

I choose to tap into and unleash the tenacious, resilient, and indomitable spirit of me?

I can dwell in the house of self-pity over my shortcomings and character flaws or I can dwell in the house of thanksgiving for my body, mind, and spirit.

My choices will shape the color of my life in vibrant shades of reds, yellows, purple, and greens, or dark clouds of smoky grays and dismal blacks.

My life experience is my choice.

I am responsible for the quality of my life.

I am not a victim of life; I am a traveler in life with choice over my own path.

I will choose gratitude, empowerment and passion.

I will choose all things positive and powerful with good intent for all mankind.

I am an insuppressible spirit, a fearless adventurer, a curious hungry traveler on the journey of my lifetime.

I am all that I need to be and choose to be.

I am perfectly imperfect, for good and perfect reason.

When you are ready, you may emerge from your relaxed state, feeling better than you did before, knowing that you are richer in mind, body, and spirit for having had this experience. And so you are.

CHAPTER SIX

Step 3: Releasing Resentment and Forgiving Others

To forgive is to set a prisoner free and discover that the prisoner was you.

—Lewis B. Smedes
Forgive and Forget: Healing the Hurts We Don't Deserve

Growing up Southern Baptist, there were a couple of biblically based social messages I heard time and time again. One was "do unto others as you would have them do unto you." The other was, "you must forgive to be forgiven." This second one proved difficult for me. As I began the emotional cleansing process in my recovery from anxiety disorder and alcoholism, I bumped up against the idea of forgiveness as a final obstacle to my emotional freedom. As much as I knew I needed to forgive, I just couldn't wrap my mind around offering someone a gift they didn't deserve, especially not the person who had hurt me most—my stepfather. Why should I give him anything? Why should I forgive him when he stole my innocence and set in motion the cycle of fear, shame, and panic I was still struggling with today? What made him deserving of my forgiveness? As I wrestled with these questions, my anger and resentment boiled and bubbled to the surface, over and over again, threatening to swamp the delicate beginnings of my hard-won peace of mind.

Anger and resentment toward others are common companions to anxiety, because the disorder often stems from experiences of victimization. Step 3 in our Escape Anxiety program will guide you through releasing these toxic feelings through learning what forgiveness is and, just as importantly, what it is not. I will show you how to forgive those who have hurt you, just as I eventually did, and liberate yourself from the negative effects of anger and resentment.

What Forgiveness Is Not

Back when I was wrestling with my own recovery, I basically thought forgiveness meant giving someone else a pass that he did not deserve. For a while, I pretended to forgive my perpetrator by trying to convince myself he didn't really mean to hurt me. But a voice inside my head just said, "B.S.! Yes, he did!" And I just couldn't get past it. I remember thinking to myself, "If I have to forgive him to get into Heaven, I just might not be able to get in."

Eventually, I began to explore what other people thought about forgiveness. I wanted to know how they got past this insurmountable obstacle, and if their experiences and insights might help me to find a way to the other side. One of the most common answers I heard from the people that I asked was a variation on this idea: "Forgiveness is a gift we give to ourselves, for our own freedom. It's not for anyone else." Well, okay. That made sense. But I still couldn't bring myself to tell my stepfather that what he did was okay, even so I could then be free.

And besides, that didn't sound like the key to freedom to me. It sounded like a duplicate key to resentment. It still seemed as though I had to do something for him that I didn't want to do—which felt like being abused all over again! After all, I wouldn't be having these problems in the first place if he hadn't abused me. Round and round I would go in my mind, and I was still stuck.

One day, I was talking to my mom about my dilemma, and she recommended a book by Lewis B. Smedes called *The Art of Forgiving*. She told me it had helped her forgive the people in her life who had hurt her. So I bought the book and it changed my life. "I have discovered that most people who tell me that they cannot forgive a person who wronged them are handicapped by a mistaken understanding of what forgiving is,"[27] he wrote. Boy, was he right about me! As I read on, I had the same experience over and over again. "He gets me, and the struggles I'm facing to find emotional freedom through forgiveness!" Here's what I learned from reading his book and embarking on my own process of forgiveness.

First, I came to understand that everyone I'd spoken to was right: forgiveness truly is a gift we give ourselves. Of course, we can offer it to someone else if we want to and it matters to them, but it is not necessary. In fact, you don't even have to tell the other person in order to forgive him. Sometimes, the person you need to forgive may be someone who has passed on, and you can do this for yourself even though she is gone.

I also learned that forgiveness is *not* the same thing as renewing, rekindling, or re-engaging in a relationship with the person you are working toward forgiving. Some may choose to reconcile with their offenders. It is not, however, a requirement for forgiving someone. This was important to me because I didn't have a single thread of intention to ever see that man again, much less reconcile and have some sort of relationship with him. This was true too for other relationships I've had in my life where I have felt wronged by other people. I was so relieved to learn that I could forgive them, but still not really want them in my life anymore because I knew that just wouldn't be a healthy choice for me.

Forgiveness is also *not* giving someone a pass or excusing the person's behavior. Some actions and behaviors are simply inexcusable. I really loved this revelation. I hadn't realized I could forgive someone and still not make any excuses for or condone their actions. Suddenly, forgiveness began to feel approachable to me. I began to feel "I can do this." I could forgive my stepfather without saying "Oh, it's okay that you molested me and I've had trouble with sex since that day." Which I was never going to say!

Lastly, I understood that forgiveness does *not* mean foregoing your right to seek justice. Justice is different from revenge. Sometimes people use the justice system to get revenge, and sometimes it makes sense to do just that. But that is not the way to emotional freedom. You can seek justice and still have emotional freedom. You may need to seek justice for your own healing, as well as for the well-being of your community. With the help of my parents, I did seek justice. Yet for many years, I still felt the need for revenge. And as I shared earlier in the book, the polygraph experience led to my first panic attack, which just threw salt on that wound. Nevertheless, I'm glad I chose to seek out the law to protect myself and others who might have encountered that man in the future.

In a situation like mine the desire for revenge is understandable, and it may be hard to separate it out from the desire for justice. But let's take a milder example to illustrate the difference. If my neighbor's teenage son decided to try out his new wheels on my front yard, I would most likely seek financial reparation for the damages. I might even have a few stern yet heartfelt words with the young man or his mother. But there wouldn't be a need for me to seek revenge. I wouldn't spend any mental time on how I might even the score with the neighbors. Learning to separate the desire for justice from the desire for revenge is critical to understanding forgiveness.

So, What *Is* Forgiveness?

Now that we understand what forgiveness is not, let's look at what it is.

Forgiveness is accepting that human nature is often fallible. As fallible humans, we hurt people, often unintentionally. In fact, many times our intentions are good but the results are poor. If you are from the baby boomer generation, you may be able relate well to this example of the well-intended yet fallible nature of humans: for many generations, parents believed that corporal punishment was the only way to discipline a child. This mindset led to many instances of unintentional child abuse, and a large part of the boomer population ended up in therapists' chairs trying to come to terms with punishment-related abuse from their childhoods. As another common example that I witnessed as an addiction specialist, and regrettably participated in as an active alcoholic, is the often-unintended harm we inflict on ourselves and others under the influence of a mind-altering substance. You don't have to be an addict or alcoholic to relate to this. Most people at some point in their lives have drunk enough alcohol to know about unintended bad behavior. Sometimes we also cause unintended harm because of damage or dysfunction in our brains.

As far as my offender goes, I am sure that something was not right in his brain. He definitely wasn't connected to the consequences of his actions, nor did he feel any compassion for how his actions might impact another human being—in my case, a child. I don't know what happened in his life that may have influenced this disconnect. But whether it was as the result of his environment or some malfunction in his brain, I could conclude that he was not a well human being, and unfortunately his demons did impact others.

We are flawed. We are imperfect. Understanding the fallible nature of human beings at a deeper level helped me to realize that although I am certain I would never, in a million years, commit the act that was committed against me, I have done harm to others and commit wrongs against others. I have hurt my mother, my children, my co-workers, and my close friends at times, through making tough business decisions, through fear-based parenting, and in moments of self-righteousness and self-centeredness. My mouth is one of my biggest offenders. I have said things both verbally and in writing that

I wish I hadn't. How many times do we wish we could suck those words right back into our mouths or un-send that sent message?

Understanding and owning my own history of poor behavior allowed me to see—and accept—the imperfect and/or impaired human nature of my offender. No excuses for him, no excuses for myself. Just fact.

Forgiveness is the realization that some people truly don't recognize that what they are doing is hurtful, while others are mentally ill or just spiritually void. It is important to remember we aren't all raised with the same moral codes. Sensitivity and compassion for others is subjective. The level of conscience varies from one human being to another. We are all coming from our own life experience. Parents who used corporal punishment didn't necessarily intend to damage their children's self-esteem and psyche into adulthood. They were just using methods passed down to them from generations before.

Here's another key reframing of forgiveness that was a game-changer for me—again, it came from that wonderful book by Lewis B. Smedes. He identified one of the fundamentals of forgiveness as being this: "We surrender our right to get even."[28] That resonated with me. Have you ever been struggling with understanding something, like algebra or how to change a tire, and suddenly felt like a huge light bulb turned on in your head? That's what happened for me when I read that sentence. That urge to "get even" or seek revenge was like a mental obsession for me. So I came up with my own version: *Forgiveness is letting go of the mental obsession with revenge.*

There were two key terms in this description for me. One was "letting go" or "surrender," as Smedes put it. This is a choice—that meant it was up to me! I had to make the decision. The other was "mental obsession." I certainly was afflicted with this! I was consumed with what happened to me. I had allowed it to define me.

When I thought about who I was, it was always at the forefront of my mind. It was if I had an unsightly scar on my face and everyone saw it, including me, before they could see the real me. I was a victim. What I was coming to realize was that if it was my choice to let go of the mental obsession, then it had been my choice to engage in the mental obsession in the first place. The painful part of this realization was seeing that it was me who was allowing my stepfather to re-injure me every time I mentally obsessed about the abuse. That's why, with the exception of telling my story of sexual abuse in this book, I rarely share it anymore. I don't want to give it any power.

It is the obsession in our minds that keeps us in the bondage of victimhood, resentment, and anger, and keeps the other person or situation in control. When I came to terms with the fact that I had done everything I could to seek justice, and that I was not going to act on any fantasy of revenge, for the first time I became willing to let go.

With every revenge script we develop in our mind regarding an event where we were offended, we are feeding the obsession consuming our souls. When I accepted I would likely never act on my desire for revenge, and that my mental fantasies were in fact holding me emotionally and spiritually captive, as I self-inflicted another form of cruelty, I became willing to let go.

To forgive, we also have to accept that we cannot change the past. Of course, we wish we could. Oh, how I had wished he hadn't done that to me. Oh, how I wished my mother had never married him. Oh, how I wished my father had better protected me and his marriage to my mother so that I wouldn't have been vulnerable to someone like my stepfather. Oh, how I wished so many things had been different. When I contemplated what it meant to let go of the mental obsession or wish to change an unchangeable past, I had another light-bulb moment. It meant I needed to simply accept that it happened. I knew it wasn't my fault. I knew I was more than that event in my life. I knew I was sick and tired of being someone's victim. I wanted to be my own victor. At that moment, I made a choice and the chains fell off. I finally knew the gift of freedom through forgiveness.

When I realized that I was actually choosing to give my offender power over my life (by allowing him to dominate the contents of my thoughts), I found the power I needed to forgive—by once and for all letting go of the anger. I understood that we have to let go of pain before we can be free of it. The power of letting go is the freedom of accepting that we can't change what happened to us, no matter how desperately we want to change it. But we can empower ourselves by changing our experience with the memory of it—by letting it go. Stop the fantasies of revenge; stop the "what if it never happened?" thinking. It is not helpful. You are in control. Holding on to anger is a choice. Choose to set yourself free. You are the answer; you are the key.

Understanding forgiveness in this way also helped me to have faith in a divine order. That faith reminds me that we will reap what we sow, and it's not my job to dole out consequences according to my personal desires.

Through coming to an understanding of what forgiveness is and isn't, driven by a willingness to go to any length to attain a peace of mind and wellness, I was finally able to work through this process and forgive my offender. I am free. And you, too, can be free. The anger no longer has any power over me. I am now able to remember the event without feeling the pain. It is a fact of my life but it doesn't define my life. What happened to me is not who I am. My past doesn't define my future. Freedom is what I desired and freedom is what I chose.

EXERCISE: *Preparing to Forgive*

To prepare yourself for the process of letting go of an obsession with getting even or a need to change an unchangeable past, I encourage you to fearlessly answer these questions. Write your answers in your journal. Only you need to know the answers. It is your freedom you seek. Your freedom is your business. I have included examples from my own story to help you.

1. What are you afraid of?

   For example: I was most afraid of giving my perpetrator something he didn't deserve and somehow sending the message to him and to the world that what he did was okay. I think there was also a part of me that was afraid of losing the "victim/survivor badge of honor." It had become a part of my identity. I also was afraid people would forget the pain I had suffered and I would lose their sympathy.

2. What has your resentment cost you?

   For example: My resentments cost me a new empowering identity as a strong, creative, and loving woman. They cost me my own power because I had given so much of my time, thoughts, energy, and future to my abuser. They cost me my joy and the opportunity to give others joy too.

3. What do you hope to gain?

   For example: I wanted to free up the space in my head for a new, healthy preoccupation. I wanted to smile again from the inside out and mean it. I wanted to be free of the emotional bondage I, and only I, had allowed him to keep me in for the past almost twenty years of my life.

The Cost of Not Forgiving

I'm not saying forgiveness is easy. It's not easy and it's not fast. It takes time. It's a process, not an event. Expect relapses and opportunities for do-overs. But when we understand the price we pay for holding on to its opposite—resentment—the effort becomes worthwhile and even desirable. I've often heard people say that holding on to resentments is like drinking poison and then wishing the other person would die. This little metaphor is even truer than first meets the eye. When we nurture resentments, our brains literally excrete a powerful concoction of stress hormones that are potentially poisonous toxins to our bodies.

I like to define resentments as the grub worms of the soul. If you don't know what a grub worm is, let's just say it's one the most grotesque creatures on earth. They dwell beneath the earth and feed on roots. They kill beautiful plants. They eventually become what are commonly known as June bugs (which, by the way, are a close second to the grub worm for the most grotesque creature award). They don't go from cocoon to beautiful butterfly; they go from gross grub worm to ugly flying bug with sticky feet. Anyway, that's how I see resentments: as grub worms that dwell beneath the surface of our minds and eat away at the roots of our spirit so that its fruits can never ripen. We can't be creative, loving, compassionate winners in this world if we are being literally eaten away by mental obsessions from our past. We have to choose one or the other.

That being said, forgiveness takes time, and it's not something you can force yourself to do before you are ready. When you've become a victim, you will go through many emotional stages before you are really ready to release the chains of resentments and even traumatization. It's important to remember that forgiveness is a process, much like the grief process. In fact, I have found that the process closely mirrors Elisabeth Kübler-Ross's famous five stages of grief, which she identified in her 1969 book *On Death and Dying*. This makes sense, because when you've been victimized, you've endured a loss—the loss of something sacred. You've lost a possession, an idea, or ideal. Perhaps it's your innocence, your safety, your peace of mind, the childhood you thought you deserved, the promise of something you now can never have. Whatever it is or was, it is profound loss.

Kübler-Ross's first stage is Denial and Isolation. This is a coping mechanism to deal with the shock of the loss. With victimization, the denial may take the form of attempts to justify the act for the other person, especially if it is someone you loved and trusted. The second stage is Anger. Anger can be expressed in many ways and in many different directions, but what it comes down to is that we were not ready for the loss. In cases of victimization, this anger is usually not directed at the offender. Many times this anger is self-destructive and its underlying motive is a cry for help. The third stage is Bargaining. This is often a frantic attempt to make sense of the loss or take responsibility for it by wondering "what if . . .?" In cases of victimization, these thoughts may go something like, "what if I had seen it coming?" or "what if I had not fallen into the trap?" The fourth stage is Depression, where the prospect of moving forward seems insurmountable. After victimization, life is now forever different. The thought of fitting into that new mold is daunting and overwhelming. The final stage is Acceptance. This is what I came to when I was able to let it go.

Understanding that forgiveness is a process that will help you give yourself the time and space you need to forgive naturally. Again, Lewis B. Smedes has great wisdom to share on this point. "I worry about fast forgivers," he writes. "They tend to forgive quickly in order to avoid their pain. Or they forgive fast in order to get an advantage over the people they forgive. And their instant forgiving only makes things worse . . . People who have been wronged badly and wounded deeply should give themselves time and space before they forgive . . . There is a right moment to forgive. We cannot predict it in advance;

we can only get ourselves ready for it when it arrives . . . Don't do it quickly, but don't wait too long . . . If we wait too long to forgive, our rage settles in and claims squatter's rights to our souls."[29]

As you move through this work, be sensitive to your own readiness. You may come to a point where you think you're ready and attempt it only to find that you've taken it back. That's okay. Just keep working at it. Forgiveness is not an event; it's a process.

When I think of all the people who are trapped in the bondage of pain and anger and resentment, I'm saddened that we are not taught these simple but profoundly life-altering coping skills. Learning to forgive was my way out; I hope it is yours too.

I'll end with a story that has always stayed with me as proof that we can forgive anything, even the most heinous crime. I was working with a patient, James, who was self-medicating his pain over the loss of his seven-year-old niece who had been brutally murdered. He attended one of my lectures on forgiveness and asked, "How can I possibly forgive this monster who maliciously, violently murdered my beautiful little niece?" Gently, I took him through the process of understanding that he was not ever going to excuse the terror that man bestowed on his precious niece. "Nothing will ever take the edge off the evil of his actions," I assured him. "There is no excuse, rhyme, or reason for what he did. It is unthinkable, unfathomable."

Then I asked him to think a minute about what kind of human being could do such a shockingly nightmarish thing. What might have happened that this human being could become such a monster? What it must have been like to be in such a wretchedly sick and demented state of mind? Eventually, he began to recognize this man must have been sick beyond anyone's understanding to have been capable of such a horrific act on a helpless little girl.

Then I asked him to share about the mental torment he had been suffering as the result of this man's actions. He talked about there not being enough booze in the world to ease his pain. He admitted he was in fact killing himself with drugs and alcohol over what this man had done and stolen from his niece. As he spoke, he began to realize that he too was falling prey to this man's murderous evil—in effect, allowing the murderer to take two lives instead of one. "James," I asked him quietly, "How deeply sad must your precious niece be to helplessly witness her beloved uncle losing his life to this monster as well?"

I could see the shock of the reality in his face. For a moment, time stood still. I wasn't sure I had said the right thing. This was the most delicate conversation I had ever had, in my entire career. "Oh my God," he said softly, eyes still glazed from the flood of new thoughts. "He is killing me and I am letting him!" Then he got angry over the power he had given to this man—the power to rob him not just of his beloved little girl, but of his life, his health, his well-being, his hope, his dreams, and his future. I could see the shift in his eyes, in his body and in his voice, as he chose to reclaim his life and began to let the chains of his deadly resentment fall away.

GUIDED MEDITATION FOR FORGIVING OTHERS

I'm honored to share this powerful guided meditation to help you let go once and for all of the chains of resentment. I have shared this meditation in groups of people suffering from unthinkable crimes against their bodies, minds, and spirits. I am humbled to have had the pleasure of witnessing profound freedom as a result. I wish you freedom too!

In preparation, write down three words that clearly represent circumstances, events, or people in your life that have held you captive with pain, anger, and resentment. For example, if anger about a past job loss plagues you, write the word "job." Or if you still burn when you think of your Dad's abandonment when you were a child, write "father." You know the scenario by heart; just use one word to describe it.

To prepare for this meditation, find a quiet place without interruption.

Convince yourself that outside noises will not disturb you. Remind yourself that this guided meditation exercise is for your highest good.

Begin by tightening your muscles as tightly as you can. Tighten your face, neck, and shoulders, and hold it. Now, tighten your arms, fingers, legs, and toes. Hold it. Now release—release completely. Allow your body to be limp and relaxed.

Take a moment here and if you choose, invite your spiritual guides, your God, or your angels to join you on this relaxation journey.

Now, take a deep breath into the fullness of your lungs.

And exhale, releasing all of the stress from your mind, body, and spirit.

Breathe in again deeply, the air of confidence and surety.

Breathe out fear and doubt.

Breathe in the air of peace and tranquility.

Breathe out all controlled thought.

Now, being conscious of your mental and physical state of relaxation, on the count of three you will double your relaxed state

One. Two. Three.

You have come here seeking true freedom from your burdens and restoration through forgiveness.

Having realized the significance of forgiveness in your quest for true freedom and everlasting peace, you fearlessly move deeper into forgiveness. Remind yourself of these words of wisdom:

As you have wronged others, so have others wronged you.

Forgiveness is not an excuse for another person's actions.

It is letting go of the mental obsession with getting even.

Above all else, forgiveness is a gift you give unto yourself.

It is your own freedom that you seek—freedom from the bondage of pain, anger and resentment.

Consider that some people know not what they do; others are of ill mind and spirit from the circumstances of their own lives.

To be free at last, you reach deep within your soul for the mercy and grace you eagerly seek for yourself.

To be free, you gather the courage to offer forgiveness without resistance.

To be free at last, you let go of the obsession with changing an unchangeable event.

To be free at last, you let go once and for all. You let it go.

Welcome and own your freedom.

Welcome and own your peace.

The emotional companions of pain, resentment, anger, and remorse are no more.

They are your companions no more.

I invite you to join me in a spiritual exercise that you may use as a tool for self-preservation and securing of the gift of your newfound freedom.

Turn to where you wrote down the three words that represent the most significant subjects that have been the core source of your burdens.

These words may be names of people, names of emotions, or names of circumstances.

Allow these three words to sit unattended at the top of your mind for now. You will come back for them later.

Now, you are walking to a quiet, beautiful, and safe place by the ocean's edge.

You can feel the grains of warm, moist sand beneath your feet.

You can feel the warmth of the sun on your shoulders and on your face.

You can feel the soft, subtle movement of the wind against your skin and through our hair.

You can hear the soft chatter of sea gulls in the distance.

You can see and hear the majesty of the movement of the ocean's water, which is home to another world of our creator's great creations.

You are warm; you are safe. You can feel the comfort of the presence of those who have gone before you—their love, support, and compassion. All of those who love you now and have gone before you are with you in spirit.

As you walk the sandy beaches, find a perfect place to sit and rest by the ocean's edge.

Allow the palms of your hands to lay open, facing upwards to the skies.

Without effort, go back to your three words and allow them to escape through the top of your head.

Watch them without moving as they tumble down your arms and into the palms of your hands. Effortlessly catch them in your hands.

Now squeeze them as tightly as you possibly can. Squeeze, squeeze and hold them.

And release.

Watch as they float up before you.

Take a deep breath.

And watch them move away from you with the release of your breath.

Breathe in again, and release with even more effort, moving them farther away from you.

Again, breathe in deeply.

Now, with the release of your breath, move them completely out of your sight.

They are no more.

You are liberated from their power over you.

You are free.

Rest in the comfort of this peaceful place.

Rest in your place of true freedom.

You have chosen it; it is yours.

Rest in your place of peace.

~~~

When you are ready, you may emerge from your relaxed state, feeling better than you did before, knowing that you are richer in mind, body and spirit for having had this experience. And so you are.

CHAPTER SEVEN

Step 4:
Surrendering Shame and Resentment
Forgiving Yourself

Shame is the lie someone told you about yourself.

—Anaïs Nin, *The Diary of Anaïs Nin*

Shame is the most insidious of emotions. Like an infection, it takes hold and festers, poisoning our thoughts with self-hatred and remorse. And for anxiety sufferers who tend to be perfectionists, shame is an almost inevitable result of every incident where we fall short of our own unrealistic expectations. We obsess over what we did or didn't do. We search for ways to cover it up through denial or blaming others, or maybe justify it by someone else's actions. We might even walk around like a whipped puppy without a voice as a demonstration of our guilt and remorse. None of these scenarios are healthy; nor will they lead you out of the oppressive emotions that elicit symptoms of chronic anxiety and panic attacks. Releasing the knot of shame and forgiving oneself is essential for lasting recovery from chronic anxiety and panic. In this chapter we'll be learning how to do this through Step 4 of the Escape Anxiety process.

As an anxiety sufferer, it was always curious to me that there was so much shame associated with anxiety. I was baffled as to why I would feel so much shame after an anxiety attack. After all,

I hadn't shown up in someone's office stark naked or told some incredibly inappropriate joke. In fact, much to the contrary. I was usually impeccably dressed in my 1980s successful-saleslady gear, equipped with an arsenal of compelling reasons why you needed to buy my handy dandy *Auto Trader* ad. Nevertheless, every time I would leave an office after experiencing even the slightest hint of anxiety symptoms, let alone a full-blown attack, I would get into my car and literally hang my head in shame and begin a seemingly endless self-inflicted, self-berating attack. "How dare you? How could you?" I'd say to myself. "That was so stupid of you to feel that way. What the hell is wrong with you?" And on and on. How's that for fostering a healthy self-esteem?

When I began researching shame in an attempt to understand why it was so closely associated with the anxiety experience, I found that the root of the word shame is thought to derive from an ancient Germanic word meaning "to cover." Something clicked immediately. That made perfect sense! Although I certainly wasn't walking into those offices naked, I did feel like I had exposed myself—exposed a part of me that I wanted to hide from others. I didn't want those car dealers to see that I was a vulnerable and scared salesgirl who needed their money. I didn't want them to know that I suffered from anxiety. I didn't want them to know that I was struggling. My ideal self was very far removed from my actual self and my anxiety attack pulled back the covers on me and exposed the truth I was so desperately trying to hide. Not only was I afraid of being rejected if anyone knew my truth, I was afraid I would lose my job, my house, my car, and my marriage. Most importantly, I was afraid that I would fall apart, forever. There's that four letter word again, *fear.*

One of the best descriptions of shame I found was from Charles Darwin in his book *The Expression of the Emotions in Man and Animals.* He described the shame symptoms as blushing, confusion of mind, downward cast eyes, slack posture, and lowered head with a sensation of heat in extreme shame situations.[30] Wow! That sounds just like the symptoms of an anxiety attack.

Another description I found enormously helpful in understanding shame came from author John Bradshaw, who made a powerful distinction between guilt and shame: "Guilt says I've *made* a mistake; shame says I *am* a mistake. Guilt says what I *did* was not good; shame says I *am* no good."[31]

The Fear-Panic-Shame Cycle

Not only does shame add to the agony of a panic attack—it actually fuels the disorder, creating a toxic cycle of fear, panic, and shame. The experience of shame after an anxiety attack is the secondary root of anxiety. Fear builds the fire pit, shame lights the fire. It is this secondary root that quickly becomes the primary root that fuels this predatory cycle. It's almost as if the fear-panic-shame cycle separates from us, becoming an independent entity that threatens our survival, stalking us, lying in wait, waiting for our most vulnerable moments to rip our masks off, to taunt and ridicule us, naked and exposed in front of our peers. It is the fear of this horrifying experience happening again that lights the flame to yet another fear-panic-shame cycle.

The cycle of these experiences, left untreated, will progress. This is the reason why it's so important to seek treatment at the first sign of these symptoms. General anxiety symptoms become anxiety disorders, panic disorder, and, in the most advanced cases, agoraphobia. Agoraphobia is a type of anxiety disorder in which you avoid places or situations that might cause you to feel panic or embarrassed. The fear is that you will be trapped with no easy way to get out or seek help if you begin to feel anxiety. The Mayo Clinic notes that "Most people who have agoraphobia develop it after having one or more panic attacks, causing them to fear another attack and avoid the place where it occurred."[32] People with agoraphobia

Step 5. Mind now thinks the mind and body are a THREAT

Step 1. THREAT (fear-based thought are imagined)

Step 2. Brain Believes the Threat is Real

Step 3. Body responds with Fight or Flight Response that equals panic

Step 4. Mind feels ashamed because body betrayed it by thinking the threat was real

The fear-panic-shame cycle

can have a hard time feeling safe in any public place and often become house-bound. The mere thought of leaving home becomes an overwhelming prospect.

Three Keys to Freedom from Shame

Now that we've established that as anxiety sufferers, we feel the great pain of shame possibly more than anyone else on earth, let's look at what the solution is. Here are the three keys to your freedom from shame:

- Acceptance of self

- Being part of a larger community

- Forgiveness of self

1. Accepting Yourself

One of my favorite passages about acceptance is found in *The Big Book of Alcoholics Anonymous* (and I'm certainly not alone in resonating with this sentiment—it's one of the most quoted passages in literature outside John 3:16 in the Bible!). It says:

> Acceptance is the answer to all my problems today. When I am disturbed, it is because I find some person, place, thing, or situation—some fact of my life—unacceptable to me, and I can find no serenity until I accept that person, place, thing, or situation as being exactly the way it is supposed to be at this moment.[33]

It seems like such a simple idea—that accepting me for me and you for you can be the key to happiness. So why do we find it so hard? Perhaps we think it's too simple to really be true. For a moment, imagine being in a state of complete acceptance. Feel the breath release from your body. Feel the chatter in your mind release its grip. What you're feeling is the sweet release of surrender.

As a therapist working in treatment, my favorite moments were those when I would witness one of my patients move into acceptance and out of denial. They would start out denying they had a problem, denying that the problem was bigger than themselves, denying that they couldn't fix it by themselves, denying the help they needed, denying that they were ill. And then a day would come when the long hard battle of attempting to control, hide, and mask their illness was finally over. I would witness easier, softer smiles. They would laugh more, share more, and cry more. The light in their eyes was lit again. They had begun the profoundly visible process of transformation.

I particularly remember one woman named Kimberly. She had recently suffered the loss of her husband of twenty years to an unexpected heart attack. Kimberly and her husband owned a very successful horse farm, and although Kimberly was quite capable of managing the farm alone, intellectually and physically, she was not prepared to handle it emotionally. So she attempted to push through her pain, skip the mourning, and get back to work. That plan was short-lived on the functioning scale. Kimberly was in denial that her husband was dead, and it hurt like hell. She was in denial that she missed him. She was in denial that she wasn't capable of carrying the burden of this loss and the farm by herself. She was attempting to repress this truth for fear that her son or one of farm hands would know she was human and most importantly, of course, for fear that if she felt at all, the pain would kill her.

Not surprisingly, these attempts failed miserably. Kimberley began to have panic attacks, which she tried to stop with vodka, thinking no one would be able to smell it on her and concern themselves with her drinking. Eventually, it was her son who suggested she get help so they could have her around a little longer. When she came to me, she was in complete denial, only showing up to satisfy her son. It took some time, but as she began to hear herself tell her own stories, she began to recognize her denial and deep desperation.

One day, she confessed to me that when things got really bad, she would hide behind her hot water heater in the basement of her beautiful grand home. As she shared this poignant and painful image, her body, mind, and spirit let go. It was profound; it was visible. She had surrendered and finally allowed me in to help her. The last time I saw her, she was enthusiastically telling me about her outings with her grandchildren. She was free.

To accept who we are we have to let go of what we once thought was right. In Kimberly's case, it was the idea she had to be a tough girl to run that farm and that to show her pain would be shameful. She had to let go of the idea that she wasn't supposed to feel her pain and deeply mourn the loss of her husband. Kimberly didn't realize until she let go and accepted herself that a new but different life was waiting her, one in which she could enjoy the company of other women who shared pain similar to her own. Life wasn't over; it was just different.

Self-forgiveness and acceptance are inherently intertwined. You can't forgive yourself until you accept yourself the way you were or are. You don't have to accept the way you will be, because if you go through the process of accepting and forgiving yourself in the past and present, you will be different in the future! I guarantee it.

2. Finding Community

When we feel shame, our natural inclination is to hide and isolate ourselves. In fact, the last thing we need to do is sit and hide! We need to go out and share. We need consciously unmask ourselves among others whom we trust, and who in turn honor our unmasking by unmasking themselves. There is nothing in the world that alleviates pain better than knowing we are not alone. As Rick Warren writes in *The Purpose Driven Life,* "Fellowship is a place of grace, where mistakes aren't rubbed in but rubbed out."[34] We are not so unique in our pain and suffering as we think we are. We have to remember that the people we encounter in our daily lives are also masking their real selves.

At Michael's House, a dual diagnosis treatment center in Palm Springs, CA, I worked in the family program. Families would come for three- or five-day intensive workshops and learn everything they could ever want to know about being an addict or loving an addict, co-dependency, their own behaviors, their loved ones' behaviors, and so on. But in the end, the most important part of their experience was always that they were able to be honest about their own and their families' uglies with other families who also shared their uglies. They were not alone.

They began to have hope that "together, we can." I think this is why Catholics flock to churches for confession—it's a place where they can be honest, with a promise of forgiveness. And it also explains why literally millions of people in the United States and abroad attend twelve-step meetings. In these meetings one person after another fearlessly shares their deepest, darkest secrets, and no one is ever rejected, no matter what the horror of their injustices to self or others. They are accepted as a *part of* a community, rather than being *apart from* others behind a shield of shame.

If you're isolated and need to find a safe place to fit in and begin your healing process, I encourage you to seek community and fellowship through your local churches or health organizations. Your local hospitals and counseling centers may offer Grief and Recovery or Divorce and Recovery classes. There are also endless types of twelve-step meetings like EA (Emotions Anonymous), CODA (Co-dependents Anonymous), Al-Anon, and so on. Trust me, there is a place for you. You just have to be willing to surrender and pick up the phone to ask for help.

3. Forgiving Yourself

When you consider the prospect of forgiving yourself so that you can be free of the shame that binds, it helps to think back to your past and remember your first experience of shame. It is this first experience that began the story you tell yourself about yourself. You have to know what the story is all about before you can begin to rewrite it. This exercise is particularly helpful so that you can make the empowering decision to re-parent your adult self differently from now on. We can see in Kimberly's story that someone, somewhere along the line sent her a message that tough girls that stuff their feelings get the job done best and anything short of that would be shameful. Clearly, that was not the best message for her after the loss of her husband.

As a part of my own recovery, I ventured back into my childhood and dug out this: my first shame experience. One evening, when I was about four years old, I was playing in the living room next to the kitchen. My brother, who is eighteen months older than me, was there too and he had a friend over. I was in a pretty hyperactive state, running around and feeling joyful, and I imagine that I was enjoying the attention I was getting from my brother and his little friend. Suddenly, my dad came over and struck me on the head with his middle finger. Hard. It hurt! "Settle down!" he ordered. Oh my gosh. The feelings rushed from the pulsing spot on the top of my head where his finger had struck me all the way down to the tips of my toes. For the very first time, I felt the intense pain of shame.

One of my clients, Shelley, shared her first memory of shame, which has some similarities to mine, although her interpretation and resulting behavior was quite different than mine. She was sitting at the dining room table where her grandmother was teaching Shelley's younger brother how to read. Shelley was on the opposite side of the table, and noticed she could read upside down. So, she started to read the words upside down out loud. This was the first time Shelley realized she had this remarkable skill and she was excited to show her grandmother and brother her talent. Suddenly, Shelley's grandmother slapped her across the face and said, "Nobody likes a show-off!" Shelley's newfound pride fell hard and heavy into a painful pit of shame.

The examples I just gave, as painful and impactful as they are, are fairly common and everyday childhood incidents of shame. The work of self-forgiveness comes in when you look at your own first shame experience and determine the blame-message you adopted from that experience that is causing you pain. The blame-message I had to forgive myself for was that I was inappropriate around boys, because my father had so abruptly stifled my behavior. From that point on, I always felt inferior and questioned my presence, appearance, and behavior around boys. My self-esteem wings had been sharply clipped. I always knew that I was equal to men in capability, except perhaps in physical strength. Yet I struggled with feeling inferior and my drive to success was often impeded by that scar left long ago.

Shelley's message was much more clear: "Nobody likes a show off." Shelley's reaction was different from mine. She made a decision to challenge her grandmother's cruel discipline by showing her! Shelley began to live a very self-destructive life that eventually would include gang activity, violence, and intravenous drug use. Today, she has forgiven herself for her shame-response and is helping other women change theirs too.

Releasing the Shame of Sexual Abuse

The experience of shame goes to a whole new level for those of us who suffered sexual trauma as children. I was astounded one day while watching the *Oprah Winfrey Show*, at something Oprah said about her personal experience with sexual abuse. It was a topic she spoke about often and openly, making a remarkable impact on raising awareness of child sexual abuse and releasing victims' shame experience just by talking about it.

On this particular day, she said something that I think only Oprah Winfrey could say on national television without hesitation or excuse. She acknowledged that there is a natural sensation of pleasure associated with molestation. She wasn't talking about violent rape, but about seductive molestation, where the perpetrator's intent is to evoke pleasure. My heart sank with the sadness of the truth and at the very same moment I felt relieved of my shame. It was normal. She was right and damn brave to say it in front of an audience of millions. The sexual parts of our bodies were made to respond with pleasure, which is what makes the act of sexual violation such a heinous crime.

More often than not, the perpetrator is someone you trusted and felt safe with. If that person then violates you, exposes you, confuses you, scares you, hurts you, and yet at the same time you may have felt pleasure from it, this creates an internal conflict that is the breeding ground for a shame that can last a lifetime and undermine future healthy experiences of sexual pleasure. As a measure of self-protection, those of us who have been sexually violated at any time in our lives, men and women alike, feel a need to mask ourselves for fear someone will know our shameful secret. The anxious pressure of suppressing this shame is palpable. If you've been a victim of sexual abuse, I hope this truth helps to loosen the chains of shame for you like it did for me.

EXERCISE: Name the Shame

As we learned earlier from John Bradshaw's definition, shame is the feeling that "I *am* bad." This is what happens when we feel shame as the result of someone else's actions that were directed towards us. This exercise is intended to acknowledge the shame elephant in the room and give it a name!

If at all possible, it will help to release the burden of your shame if you can tell someone you trust about it. I suggest choosing someone who is neutral in life, meaning that you are not emotionally connected to that person. For example, you might choose a counselor, a clergy member, or a sponsor. There is an emotional magic that happens when we share our shame with someone else who will not judge us.

However, it's also important to learn to tell yourself about the parts of you that you keep hidden, and to learn to listen to yourself with compassion and non-judgment. In order to practice this, I'm going to ask you to step into the role of parent for yourself for a moment. Imagine what you, as a parent, would say to yourself, if you were a child? Write your answers in your journal.

Imagine that your child-self said to your parent-self, "I need to tell you about the first time I felt shame." What would you tell that child?

Then if your child-self said to your parent-self, "I need to tell you—I'm not perfect," what would you tell that child?

Then if your child-self said to your parent-self, "I need to tell you, I hate X, Y, or Z about myself," what would you tell that child?

What would you say to that child, who just revealed her soul to you? Would you shame her and send her to her room? Or would you invite her to sit on your lap and tell her all the wonderful things you know about her?

Now, write down the new messages you want to adopt from your parent self.

EXERCISE: Name the Guilt

Guilt is related to shame, but is different. As Bradshaw said, guilt is the feeling that "I've *done something* bad." And sometimes, we do indeed do bad things. To free yourself from guilt and forgive yourself for wrongs you have done, you may need to make amends with other people. Let's take a closer look at what you are feeling guilty about. Choose one particular situation, and then ask yourself these questions:

First, were your actions deliberate or accidental? (Were your actions intended to cause harm?)

Were you actually responsible for the event? (Did you actually do it, or do you just feel as if you could have or should have prevented it?)

If so, what are your feelings about it? (For example, remorse or guilt.)

Can you make an amends for it without causing additional harm? (For example, a verbal or written apology, or a "living amends," which means committing to yourself that you will not repeat the behavior.)

Is this behavior something you continue to do? (For example, having an affair or engaging in an addiction.)

Can you get help for your behavior? (For example, counseling or treatment.)

Why do you feel like you're holding on to your guilt?

Now you are ready to take action. Unfortunately, as we discussed in chapter four, when discussing Step 1 of the Escape Anxiety program, many of us tend to spend an enormous amount of time in our heads, thinking and worrying about things we have no control over, and they end up having control over us. Worrying about things we don't have any control over is exhausting and anxiety provoking! When it comes to things you feel guilty about, you can use the Know Your Cans exercise we learned in chapters four and five to separate out the things you can change from things you can't, and then take action on the things you can. Take one example at a time, and let's go back to the two columns: "Can NOT Change" and "CAN change."

Can NOT Control	CAN Control

Some examples would be:

I cannot change the pain I have already caused another person.

I can make amends in a loving and sincere way.

I cannot change the time I have lost of feeling guilty about what I've done.

I can change my thoughts, feelings, and actions today.

Based on what you put in your "CAN Change" column, make some conscious choices and move forward with the business of making amends. Giving yourself a time limit to accomplish this will help in getting it done. If you need to tell some you're sorry for your behavior, make a commitment to do it this week. If you're going to change your mind about yourself and let go your shame and guilt, make a commitment to use this mantra (a simple phrase you can repeat to yourself) over the next few days to help you. Tell yourself: *"I am forgiven, I am free, I am in the now and moving forward without old baggage. I choose to be happy, joyous, and free."*

This process is often referred to as cleaning up the wreckage of the past. Now that you've cleaned house, it is a good idea from this day forward to try to make any necessary amends to yourself or others as quickly as possible after an event happens so that you don't start stacking up guilt, shame, and remorse again.

IMPORTANT NOTE: *If you are engaging in something that you are feeling guilty about, such as excessive drinking, raging, gambling, or unhealthy sexual behaviors, you may want to seek professional help to overcome these self-destructive habits. It's okay to ask for help. I assure you, whatever it is, you are not alone and help is available. You will not be able to forgive yourself for something you know you will do again. Log onto my website (EscapeAnxiety.com) for professional resources for healing and recovery.*

GUIDED MEDITATION
FOR FORGIVING YOURSELF

This meditation is designed to help you release yourself from the bonds of shame and forgive yourself.

~~~

To prepare for this meditation, find a quiet place without interruption.

Convince yourself that outside noises will not disturb you. Remind yourself that this guided meditation exercise is for your highest good.

Begin by tightening your muscles as tightly as you can. Tighten your face, neck, and shoulders, and hold it. Now, tighten your arms, fingers, legs, and toes. Hold it. Now release—release completely. Allow your body to be limp and relaxed.

Take a moment here and if you choose, invite your spiritual guides, your God, or your angels to join you on this relaxation journey.

Now, take a deep breath into the fullness of your lungs.

And exhale, releasing all of the stress from your mind, body, and spirit.

Breathe in again deeply, the air of confidence and surety.

Breathe out fear and doubt.

Breathe in the air of peace and tranquility.

Breathe out all controlled thought.

Now, being conscious of your mental and physical state of relaxation, on the count of three you will double your relaxed state.

One. Two. Three.

You now find yourself walking in a beautiful valley, in a field of green.

The grass beneath your feet is soft and moist. You are safe and secure and at complete peace on your journey through the field toward the base of a small mountain.

You are comforted by the bird songs you hear in the distance.

It is a fresh fall morning. The trees greet you with a beautiful display of rich colors.

You are awed by nature's impeccable timing and flare for dramatics as it introduces and escorts in yet another beautiful new season.

The air is warmed by the sun's luminous rays. You are comforted by the soft breeze brushing against your skin.

You have reached the base of the small mountain and have found the path that has been cleared for your journey.

You have come here today willing to climb to higher places for higher learning. You are happy to be here, ready and eager to reach the gifts that await.

Your climb is surprisingly easy—it is almost as if you are floating.

Your breath is easy; your steps are sure.

Having tapped into your adventurous soul, amazed by your tenacious and courageous spirit, you move farther and farther up the mountain, each step fueled with more energy and curiosity than the one before.

Step, reach, and breathe.

Step, reach, and breathe.

You have come a long way and have found the top of the mountain. There is a perfect clearing and a soft, safe place to rest.

Sit, rest, breathe, and absorb.

Remind yourself of these words of wisdom:

Forgiveness of self is a choice to stop the self-inflicted pain of reliving the pain you caused yourself and others.

Forgiveness of self is moving from a past that cannot be changed to a future of new opportunities with a compassionate heart.

Forgiveness of self is a willingness to make direct amends wherever possible and a living amends from this day forward.

Forgiveness of self is having a humble heart about the errors of our past, not a broken spirit.

Forgiveness is letting go.

Letting go is freedom from a self-inflicted bondage to the unchangeable past.

Mourning past errors doesn't prevent future mistakes.

Forgiveness of self is offering yourself the grace you would so willing offer to someone else you love.

Forgiveness of self is loving yourself into mental and emotional freedom from an unchangeable past.

Forgiveness of self is a choice to move forward, to live in the now.

Forgiveness of self is accepting your own request to be forgiven.

Forgiveness of self is once and for all letting it go, never to revisit it again. It is gone, it is over, it cannot be repeated, changed, or altered in any way.

Free yourself once and for all.

Let it go.

Imagine before you a bucket. Imagine all of your past mistakes, regrets, actions, and words that you are ashamed of are like reels of film stored in your mind. They are holding you back. They are getting in the way of you living the life you want and deserve.

Pick them up, one by one, each and every one of them.

Put them all in the bucket. The bucket is big enough to hold them all. Do you have all of them? Are all of the reels of film in your mind completely cleaned out?

Be sure to the get the very last one of them. You have held on to them for too long.

They have rotted and need to be thrown out.

Get that last one, good!

You've done it. All of your past errors are in the bucket. Now, close the lid on the bucket, and seal it good so none of them can get out.

Hear the lid close as it makes its final click.

Now you are ready to put your bucket in a fiery incinerator and burn your past regrets, shame, guilt and remorse.

This is incinerator is a special incinerator, not only will it melt your bucket and all of its contents; it will transform your melted bucket into a fireball of positive, powerful energy.

Place you bucket in the incinerator. Don't wait—do it quickly, and then close the door, make sure it is secure and flip the switch.

It is burning it up at an unbelievable temperature.

Watch as the newly transformed positive powerful energy is shooting like fireworks out of the top of the chimney—vibrant, explosive blinding white light shooting up in all directions. It is breathtaking to watch the display of positive energy that was created from your own stagnant mental matter. It's incredible. It's a miracle.

You did it!

You are finally free!

Breathe and enjoy your freedom.

You chose it; own it; it is yours.

Breathe and be free!

~~~

When you are ready, you may emerge from your relaxed state, feeling better than you did before, knowing that you are richer in mind, body and spirit for having had this experience. And so you are.

CHAPTER EIGHT

Step 5:
Defusing Catastrophic Thinking

How much pain have cost us the evils
which have never happened.

—Thomas Jefferson
Letter to John Adams, April 8, 1816

If you're an anxiety sufferer, you know all too well how much real pain can arise from imagined evils. Chances are, you spend a lot of time thinking about what *could* happen. And I'm not talking about positive scenarios! Do you spin disaster movies in your head, tumbling from "what if?" to "what if?" in an ever-escalating sequence of potential horrors? Do you worry obsessively about the future? This is what's known as "catastrophic thinking." It's something most human beings fall prey to at one time or another, but anxiety sufferers are catastrophic thinkers *par excellence*. We have turned imagining the worst into a fine art. Step 5 in the Escape Anxiety program will show you how to get a handle on this tendency and keep your mind under control.

When Worry Doesn't Work

Catastrophic thinking is really just worry on steroids. It's the runaway mind-train that starts the anxiety ball rolling to an inevitable panic destination. I've also heard it called the "magical magnifying mind." A friend once told me, "Worry is praying for what you don't want to happen." We could also say that worry is a form of meditation. Any time we have focused concentration on something specific, it is a kind of meditation and/or hypnosis. So be careful what you meditate on!

For example, if you are constantly worried about losing your job, this will soon become a source of distraction, which could lead to a lack of productivity, stress in relationship with your boss, an avoidance of the boss rather than building that relationship, and so on—all of which will make it much more likely that you will, in fact, lose your job. Your worry becomes a self-fulfilling prophecy.

I love the popular saying that goes something like, "Whether you think you can or you think you can't, you are probably right." Just as athletes use the power of the mind to be the best at their sport, anxiety sufferers unwittingly use the power of the mind to be the best worrywarts around! Looking back at my life, I realize I had always feared that I would somehow end up in a psychiatric institution like my aunt Suzie. Well, I did! Most likely, when I began to be overwhelmed and stressed out about my life circumstances, somewhere in my subconscious mind I began to surrender to the growing pain of my mental anguish and think, "Well, here it is. It finally got me. I knew it would and sure enough here it is."

With all things that we humans over-use and abuse, there is usually a positive purpose somewhere in there, and catastrophic thinking is no exception. Believe it or not, there is a purpose for the human tendency toward "mental scripting" or "future tripping." It is a way of testing problem-solving approaches for potential problems that we might face in our lives. Dream analysts believe we even do this in our sleep. Author Joyce Meyers calls it "having a ready mind."[35]

For example, when you are lying in bed thinking about what might happen if you were robbed while you sleep, you go through a script in your head for how you will react if this event actually happens. Or if you're worrying about what would happen if a fire breaks out, you might plan how you would escape, and decide what you would grab to take with you. These kinds of catastrophic thinking actually help you to be ready in the event of one of these unfortunate tragedies. To some extent, it's natural to think about things that *could* happen and imagine how we would deal with them. But we get in trouble when we spend too much time doing it.

To understand why catastrophic thinking is so bad for our mind and body, let's go back to what we discussed in chapter one. Remember the fight or flight response, which triggers the release of those power-packed chemicals known as stress hormones, giving you superhuman strength and speed? And remember how Hans Selye discovered that this response can be triggered by imaginary threats as well as real ones? Well, that's what happens when you get on the runaway mind-train of catastrophic thinking. You flood your body with chemicals it doesn't really need, since there is no real threat to fight or run from, creating a toxic buildup that can lead to anxiety and panic attacks.

Catastrophic thinking can lead to phobias, which the American Psychiatric Association defines as "excessive and persistent fear of a specific object, situation, or activity." People who suffer phobias go to great lengths to avoid the object of their fear, in a way that is typically disproportional to the actual danger posed. For example, one day I was working at the Betty Ford Center, conducting a psychological assessment of a new patient. At some point, I asked him if he had a history of phobias and he said yes—he had a phobia of needles. Well, as it turns out, that became a significant problem because as a community treatment center, we had to draw blood from every patient.

This man was a big, rugged type of guy who looked like he could wrestle crocodiles with his bare hands, yet he was terrified of needles—so much so that he left treatment. When I probed the sources of his phobia, he admitted that after seeing a horror film as a child, he couldn't see a needle without spinning into scenarios where the nurse freaked out and stabbed him in the neck with a needle filled with a deadly serum, or where air would get trapped in the needle and cause him death. Fortunately, in his case, he was able to work with a therapist to get over this fear and he eventually returned to treatment.

Other common phobias include fear of spiders, elevators, highways, airplanes, and germs, and, for anxiety sufferers whose anxiety has progressed a long way, agoraphobia. I worked with a woman, Beverly, who had at one point been housebound for ten years with agoraphobia. She was only released from her fear when someone told her that soy protein could cause anxiety. It turned out that soy had been her primary source of protein for many years. When she stopped eating it, she was immediately relieved of her fear of leaving the house. Was it all created by what she ate? I don't know. Diet can play a significant role in anxiety (as discussed in appendix three), but I wasn't able to find a definitive study as to whether or not soy protein causes anxiety. However, it could have been true for her, and what was more important was that she believed it did. Eliminating this from her diet allowed her to be free of her anxiety symptoms and the debilitating agoraphobia that had held her hostage in her own home for a decade.

Addicted to Thought

These types of fears and phobias demonstrate the power of thought over the mind and body. I might go so far as to say that thoughts could be described as addictive, particularly negative ones. Now, my medical colleagues may cringe when I suggest this, because addiction is a diagnosis, and something can't be classified as an addiction if it's not in the *Diagnostics Statistical Manual of Mental Disorders.* I concur, so I will simply say that thought has addictive characteristics. Let me show you what I'm talking about by taking a look at some of the clinical criteria for Substance Use Disorder. For the purposes of this demonstration, I crossed out "substance" and replaced it with "obsessive fear or worry." See how many addiction criteria you would meet for obsessive fear or worry if it were categorized as an addiction. Keep in mind that to qualify for a substance-use disorder, you only have to meet three of the criteria.

1. ~~Taking the substance~~ (engaging in obsessive fear or worry) in larger amounts or for longer than you meant to

2. Wanting to cut down or stop ~~using the substance~~ (engaging in obsessive fear or worry) but not managing to

3. Spending a lot of time getting, using, or recovering from (engaging in obsessive fear or worry) ~~use of the substance~~

4. Cravings and urges to ~~use the substance~~ (engage in obsessive fear or worry)

5. Not managing to do what you should at work, home or school, because of ~~substance use~~ (obsessive fear or worry)

6. Continuing to ~~use~~ (engage in obsessive fear or worry) even when it causes problems in relationships

7. Giving up important social, occupational or recreational activities because of ~~substance use~~ (obsessive fear or worry)

8. ~~Using substances~~ (Engaging in obsessive fear or worry) again and again, even when it puts you in danger

9. Continuing to ~~use~~ (engage in obsessive fear or worry), even when you know you have a physical or psychological problem that could have been caused or made worse by ~~the substance~~ (obsessive fear or worry)[36]

As discussed in chapter three, what science understands today about the thought process is that if you have a deeply embedded thought pattern, your brain has created very real circuit pathways for this train of thought, which is why it's so hard to change thought habits. It can be done though. It just takes awareness and practice, practice, practice.

EXERCISE: Accidental Pie

I love this exercise and used it for years with my patients so they could get a clear snapshot of their own brain chemistry based on the idea that thought is chemical. It's an opportunity to create a map of your thought life and subsequent emotions.

Imagine your thoughts and emotions are the ingredients that you bake into the pie of your brain chemistry: a dash of obsessive worry here, a cup of self-doubt, a pinch of gratitude and a splash of hope, a few ounces of fear and dread. What kind of pie are you baking?

Grab a piece of paper and draw a great big circle.

Now, I'm going to give you two categories to choose from without getting too technical: Good Chemical Thoughts/Emotions and Negative Chemical Thoughts/Emotions.

Gratitude and Peace

Hope and Joy

Positive
10%

Positive
9%

Negative
58%

Negative
23%

Anger and
Self Doubt

Worry and Fear

*Your Daily Pie Chart will give you a good idea about what
kind of Brain Chemistry you are choosing with your daily
thoughts and highlight areas of improvement.*

This is a great exercise to do as a family!

Your Daily Thought-Life Pie Chart

Good Chemical Thoughts/Emotions

Peace, joy, compassion, acceptance, awe, wonderment, gratitude, hopefulness, peace, excitement, funny, forgiveness, kindliness, mercy, understanding, and generosity.

Negative Chemical Thoughts/Emotions

Anger, resentments, fear, jealousy, low-self esteem, negative self-talk, worry about the future, tension, desperation,
stress, torment, upset, dread, and self-pity.

Now, imagine that your circle is a pie and start drawing
pie slices that represent how much time in your day is spent
in these types of emotional thoughts.

Most of the people that I have treated over the years consistently have had a 70/30 or 80/20 pie. 70–80 percent is
spent in fear and worry-based thoughts and emotions and
20–30 percent is spent in positive thoughts and emotions.
This is how we accidentally create our own anxiety and
depression and bake them into the pie we eat every day!

EXERCISE: Make a Date with Yourself

1. Make an appointment with yourself to worry. That's
   right. Decide what your worry time is going to be
   and how much time you'll spend on it. For example,
   tonight at 6:00 pm, I'm going to worry about everything I can think of for thirty minutes. This exercise will help you be more conscious of what you're
   thinking about rather than just being a victim to your
   habitual patterns of thought. Most of us don't think
   about what we're thinking about and ever fewer of us
   know the impact of thought on our being.

2. Take time out of your day to spend a full fifteen minutes in awe and wonderment. That's right, focus on
   something you find amazing and beautiful that gives

you a childlike sense of joy and wonder. This exercise helps you to consciously trigger the release of restorative brain chemicals that naturally counterbalance stress hormones like cortisol and adrenaline. Medicine, nature's way!

GUIDED MEDITATION FOR DEFUSING CATASTROPHIC THINKING

To prepare you for overcoming obsessive catastrophic thinking, write down up to three words that represent your most disturbing catastrophic scripts. For example, you might write down the word "bridge" if you think losing your job will result in living under that freeway overpass; or "funeral" if the loss of a loved one is constantly playing in your head. It is not necessary to write the entire scenario out—you know the script pretty well by now. Just use one word to identify the mental script that is bothering you.

~~~

To prepare for this meditation, find a quiet place without interruption.

Convince yourself that outside noises will not disturb you. Remind yourself that this guided meditation exercise is for your highest good.

Begin by tightening your muscles as tightly as you can. Tighten your face, neck, and shoulders, and hold it. Now, tighten your arms, fingers, legs, and toes. Hold it. Now release—release completely. Allow your body to be limp and relaxed.

Take a moment here and if you choose, invite your spiritual guides, your God, or your angels to join you on this relaxation journey.

Now, take a deep breath into the fullness of your lungs.

And exhale, releasing all of the stress from your mind, body, and spirit.

Breathe in again deeply, the air of confidence and surety.

Breathe out fear and doubt.

Breathe in the air of peace and tranquility.

Breathe out all controlled thought.

Now, being conscious of your mental and physical state of relaxation, on the count of three you will double your relaxed state

One. Two. Three.

You are now walking in a beautiful field of green on a warm spring day. You can feel the moist green grass caressing your feet with each gentle step you take.

Feel the warm sun on your shoulders and a nice soft breeze against your skin and moving through your hair.

You are at complete peace and overcome with a sense of gratitude for the opportunity to be at one with the beauty and the wonder of the earth.

You can hear the trickling of a brook just ahead. You are drawn to the poetic sounds of the playfully flowing waters, moving over, around, and under the smooth polished rocks, large and small.

As you reach the babbling brook, you are awed by the simple beauty of Earth's innocence, unaware of your presence. The brook is a continuous glistening wellspring of calming sounds and mesmerizing images of purity and beauty.

The waters are clean and clear, happily moving down the natural path created by their flow.

Watch as the leaf rides the waves with confidence and surety, happy to be going on a new and exciting adventure.

Watch as it rides and glides up, over, and around the slippery, wet rocks. It is moving farther and farther down the stream, until finally it is gone completely from your sight.

You have come here in order to conquer the old habits of unpleasant thought patterns.

You desire to increase the quality of your life experience and obtain true peace of mind.

It is true that your life experience is a direct reflection of the contents of your thoughts.

You are the sole party responsible for the contents of your mind—the direction of your thoughts, and your perceptions of the words you hear, the events you see, the memories you choose to replay.

Your mind is our own theatre. You own all of the film. You choose which film plays, what it plays, how it sounds, what the storyline is, and what the ending is.

You choose your characters, their roles, their motives, their words, actions, thoughts, and reactions.

You choose the location of the film—indoors, outdoors, on the ground, in the sky, below the ground, beyond the sky.

You are the casting agent, stage designer, director, scriptwriter, filmmaker, and actor.

The theater of your mind has infinite potential.

You are responsible for its creative design and content. Your life is a direct reflection of your mental choices.

You get to choose the stories that are told in the theater of your mind.

The theater of your mind is a magical place with limitless potential for you to create and visualize.

You choose your life experience by the contents of your mind you choose to activate.

When you play back memories from your past, you get to choose which memories you play. Are they happy, are they sad, are they tragic, are they playful, thrilling, exhilarating, motivating, or perhaps depressing, scary or funny?

What kind of life experience are you choosing when you choose the reruns of your life?

When you play a rerun, you must ask if you have the opportunity to view it from a different perception.

Can you view the actions of your characters from a perspective of pity rather than contempt?

When you play a rerun, can you choose to view it with compassion rather than condemnation?

When you play a rerun, are you choosing to be inspired by the story rather than deflated by it?

You can change the way you look at your memories; you can change the way you experience them simply by changing your perception. It is time to choose a new perception and alter your own life experience in a positive powerful way.

When you ponder over your future, you have the same choices.

Do you imagine your day by imagining yourself traveling through your day with confidence, being aware of your capabilities and your adventurous spirit?

Are you creating expectations of your days that are achievable, that are in alignment with your commitment to have peace of mind?

Your thoughts are powerful; your thoughts are a creative force in your life.

Choose powerful positive thoughts.

Choose to see yourself as a prepared, competent, ready traveler on the journey of your life.

Choose to view yourself as a curious student of the universe, fascinated by the possibilities of life.

Do you have a sparkle in your eye that reflects the awe and wonder of the world in which you see?

Do you step lightly into your day as a fearless, courageous student of life?

Are you generous with your positive spiritual energy? Are you friendly, understanding, patient, kind and loving?

Make these words your own words:

I am less concerned about me and more concerned about you.

I will look for opportunities to comfort rather than to be comforted.

I will look for opportunities to inspire rather than to be inspired.

I will look for opportunities to encourage rather than be encouraged.

I will seize and respond to every opportunity to give rather than receive.

I will greet my day with excited anticipation for the opportunity to shed my light of joy on another life traveler.

When you are ready, you may emerge from your relaxed state, feeling better than you did before, knowing that you are richer in mind, body, and spirit for having had this experience. And so you are.

CHAPTER NINE

Step 6:
Mastering Self-Regulation

If you don't manage your emotions,
then your emotions will manage you.

—Doc Childre and Deborah Rozman, *Transforming Anxiety*

When you were growing up, do you remember your mom telling you something along the lines of, "if you get mad, hold your breath and count to ten?" Mine certainly did. Or did your parents or teachers use "time outs" to discipline you? If so, you've already learned one of the most important tools for managing your anxiety and stopping the physical reaction to the runaway mind-train. In Step 6 of the Escape Anxiety program, I will be teaching you the grown-up version of taking a time out: the simple but powerful tool of Self-Regulation.

Self-regulation simply means bringing back under control the intense, seemingly involuntary, physical reactions we have to intensely emotional thoughts. It allows you to shift from what I will call an impulsive, unconscious *reaction* to a considered, rational *response*. When we react blindly to events, whether real or imagined, we are not thinking rationally about what would be the most appropriate course of action. However, when we have the mental space to respond, that means we can think it through just long enough to assess the situation and decide what is the best course of action (which might be no action at all). Of course, there are times when spontaneous reactions are quite appropriate, but it's important to also have the ability to delay or suspend those spontaneous reactions as needed. What I distinguish as responding rather than reacting is best accomplished when you are able to set aside your own emotions in order to have more clarity about how to best deal with the situation at hand.

We are constantly bombarded with a wide variety of stimuli in our daily lives: television, traffic, advertisements on the highway, family, friends, co-workers, even the clock on the wall that ticks away all day. We are continually reacting, responding, or not to every stimulus we encounter. The goal would be to do a whole lot more responding than reacting, and this takes practice!

The illustration on page 171 is an example of what the chain of reactions/responses looks like.

The ultimate experience of emotional disregulation is a panic attack. It feels like it is going to escalate to the point of imminent death. A comforting truth about anxiety however is that it will peak and then it will come down. It will not peak and kill you and it will not peak and stay there. It always comes down. If not treated it will continue the cycle of ups and downs but down will always come.

Having the knowledge and tools to be able to bring your emotions down faster will enable you to stop a panic attack from occurring as the result of anxiety symptoms or you will be able to stop a panic attack faster once one has begun. The best option, of course, is to self-regulate your emotions at the very first sensation of anxiety.

Learning to Self-Regulate

With regard to coping with everyday life stressors, the goal is to avoid getting too emotionally high or too emotionally low. I don't know about you, but I can get really emotionally high when something gives me an indication I'm going to get something I've wanted for a long time—like when someone of affluence tells me I've got a

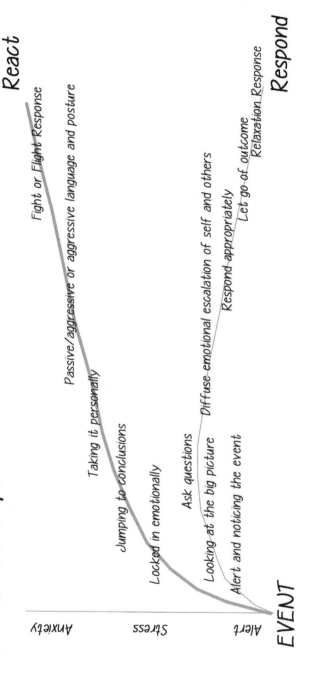

Reaction versus Response

great business idea. Within seconds, I'm on the way to the bank in my mind. Likewise, I can get just as low when someone of affluence tells me I don't have all the pieces of my business idea together to go anywhere with it. I'm suddenly standing in the unemployment line, in my mind. These kinds of highs and lows trigger a need to self-soothe. If we don't have the tools to do this naturally, the impulse is to reach for a quick fix to soothe our emotions, such as a drink, a pill, or a hit. So we need to learn how to regulate ourselves without the aid of a mind-altering substance.

This brings us back to my mom's advice. It turns out she was right. The one component necessary to begin the process of changing our reactions to our environments or the people we encounter throughout our lives is the ability to put space between an event (either an external event or an internal thought or feeling) and our response to it. I always find this amusing in its simplicity, but it is also profound. This critical space of time allows us the mental space to make a conscious choice about how we are going to deal with a situation. Our first impulses are often wrong. We need to "think" before we "react."

This is why there is such genius in the simplicity of the "time out" theory (which, by the way, was developed in the 1950s by Arthur Staats, through working with his own children). It allows the child to calm down, which in fact teaches the child that he/she *can* calm down without the parent yelling or forcing a certain behavioral response. Equally important, as many parents will attest, is the unintended time out opportunity for the parents, which allows them to calm their feelings of anger toward the child and replace yelling with a calmer and firm yet loving response to inappropriate behavior.

The Power of Breath

The simplest and most powerful tool for self-regulation—for inserting that space between trigger and reaction—is your breath.

Focusing on your breath, even for a moment, allows you the time to make a conscious decision about what just happened and what the best way is to respond to what just happened, rather than making an assumption and reacting irrationally to something you haven't confirmed as being truth. The simple instruction "take a deep breath" can make all the difference between an unconscious reaction and a considered response. For example, your son might say, "Mom, I didn't have time to take out the trash this morning." If you're not self-regulating, you might interrupt with an angry reaction before checking two things: (1) What was the reason he didn't have time? And (2) Did someone else take the trash out so it did not miss the trash pickup? That all-important deep breath allows you to process what you heard so you can realize, "I need more information about this," rather than reacting before you've heard the whole story.

This process of asking for more information to avoid escalating an event based on an assumption is closely related to the skills taught in Cognitive Behavioral Therapy. CBT, which I introduced in chapter three, is all about challenging the message to see if what you think or what you heard is real so you can respond appropriately.

Regulating Escalating Emotions

Another way to self-regulate the body by overriding what's going in the mind is to use some very simple yet profoundly effective skills commonly practiced in Dialectical Behavior Therapy (DBT). Let's say you discovered that the trash removal company missed your trash pick-up, and it was the second week in a row that your son missed the day, so the bin is full. You can feel your pulse begin to race and your face begin to get tense. Anger is on the rise. Yet, you are at the office and cannot allow your emotions to get out of control. A great DBT recommended intervention would be to grab a piece of ice and hold it in one hand. It is amazing how well this works. You will find it difficult to keep your focus on what you're angry about.

It is a perfect way to cause an immediate interruption in escalating emotions. Creating an intense physical sensation can divert the mind from its anxiety and hold its attention. Other examples might be grasping a comb tightly in your hand or squeezing a stress ball.

Focusing on the Moment

The skill that I love for distracting the sensations of anxiety is intense focus. This is at the heart of the practice of mindfulness meditation, which was discussed in chapter three. The term "mindfulness" originates in the Pali term *sati*, whose root meaning is "to remember." It signifies presence of mind, the attentiveness to the present. It draws the attention away from the projecting of fear or anger and solidly grounds us in the present, which is calming. Being in the moment allows for centeredness, clarity, and, most importantly, an appropriate emotional and behavioral response to the messages in our environment.

EXERCISE: Minding the Body

This simple exercise will help you feel the benefits of mindfulness meditation. Relax into your chair or on your bed or wherever you're sitting at the moment. Take a couple of cleansing breathes. Now, begin at the top of head by just simply noticing what your head feels like—what does your scalp feel like? What does your brain feel like? You may feel completely relaxed or you may feel some tension. Whatever it is that you feel, just notice it. Resist the temptation to analyze it or engage in thought about it in any way. Just notice and acknowledge and gently move your awareness onto your face, neck, shoulders, and slowly all the way down to your toes.

At each area of your body that you come to, repeat the process of noticing what you're feeling without "thinking" about it. Use that teflon mind analogy. Just notice, check, move on, don't attach any thought to it. Now, shift your awareness to the room you are in. First, notice what it feels like to be sitting in the chair you are in or lounging on the couch or bed. Just notice what it feels like to have the feel of fabric or wood against your skin. Now notice what it feels like to have your body supported completely by the furniture you are resting in. Now shift your awareness to the sounds and smells in the room. Just notice, don't think about them. Notice that you can shift your awareness gently from one sound to the other.

This is a very common exercise practiced in group therapy. It seems incredibly simple and maybe even silly. However, this simple skill of noticing without thinking trains us to do more observing in our environments without reacting. And that is a life-altering skill for those who suffer with anxiety.

Other Tools for Self-Regulation

No matter what you choose, it is important for you to find the best technique to remove yourself from stress and eliminate it at the source. Perhaps listening to a certain song grounds you and allows you to focus on reducing worry. Maybe deep breathing or sensory deprivation (like sitting in the dark or in complete silence) helps you to find your center. Prayer, yoga, writing, and laughter are all commonly used relaxation techniques that may work for you. Finding your personal coping skills toolbox is the key to managing your anxiety in situations that are less than ideal.

Stopping the Runaway Mind-Train: The I.R.S. Tools

I've created a simple set of tools for self-regulation, incorporating several of the techniques discussed above, that I call the I.R.S. Tools. Yes, I know you probably associate those initials with creating anxiety rather than stopping it! But in this case, I.R.S. stands for Interrupt, Redirect, and Self-Regulate. When you learn how to interrupt, redirect, and self-regulate your emotions and thoughts while you are feeling panic or anxiety, you will begin to take back control of your life. There is an old spiritual saying that the mind is a wonderful servant but a terrible master. You'll find out just how true this is when you learn to use these tools and get the upper hand over your mind, and are no longer being mentally and emotionally held hostage by the fear of another panic attack.

The best time to deploy these techniques is when you first begin to feel a sense of anxious discomfort. Sometimes, however, anxiety attacks come on so quickly that you may have to catch them midstream. That's okay, the tools will still work. The earlier you deploy them, the less damage you will do to yourself and others. I'm sure you've heard that thoughts become words; words become actions; actions become habits; and habits become character. To leave chronic anxiety and panic attacks behind, you have to make a conscious decision, right here and now, that you have choice over your thoughts. You are not the victim of your thoughts; you are the gatekeeper. With your I.R.S. tools, when you have uninvited thoughts, you will be able to immediately escort them out.

EXERCISE: Using the I.R.S Tools

Preparation: If you're experiencing frequent anxiety attacks, it's a good idea to wear a rubber band around your wrist. You'll find out why in Step 1 of the process.

Step 1: Interrupt. Suspend unwanted, scary, catastrophic thoughts the instant you recognize them. You are the boss. As soon as you feel an attack coming on, interrupt the thought process. This is where your rubber band comes in. Snap it against your wrist. The sudden sensation of pain from the snap does two things. One, it interrupts the stubborn anxiety thought process your mind is caught in. Two, it causes the immediate release of endorphins, which are naturally occurring pain-relieving chemicals in the brain, producing an immediate calming effect on the mind and body. If you find yourself without a rubber band, just give yourself a firm, quick, sharp pinch.

For example, let's say you have a fear of crossing bridges (gephyrophobia). As you approach the bridge, your mind starts chattering at you. "What if it's structurally unsound? It could crack when I'm halfway across and then I'd plummet into the river . . . I wonder how deep that water is? Would anyone save me before I drowned? I can't do this. Oh no, I'm going to freak out . . ." STOP! Snap the band. Interrupt the thought immediately. Don't even let yourself finish a sentence, much less the whole disaster-movie script. You are not going to freak out. Remind yourself that you are not a victim of your thoughts. You have a choice and your choices will determine your life experience.

I concede that this is no small feat, and it will take time to overcome these types of habitual thought patterns. It's our natural inclination to want to finish a thought process once it's begun—especially one that is scary (and, frankly, a little self-indulgent). When you are in a panic, things tend to happen so quickly that you may not be aware of the mechanics involved in the thought process. This is the greatest challenge: become aware of the mechanics, understand and dissect them. Once you understand the mechanics of the script, you will easily be able to interrupt the process and then move on to the next step, which is to redirect your thoughts to a new, more pleasant storyline.

Step 2: Redirect. Now that you've interrupted the thought, you need to anchor your attention somewhere else. Focus intensely on something else, like your breath. Slow it down and ground yourself, immerse yourself in the sensation of what it feels like to breath. Or you could focus on something in your physical environment, like the pattern on the wallpaper. To go back to our example above, you might focus on the stripe in the middle of the road leading to the bridge, or the other cars ahead of you.

Step 3. Self-Regulate. Now that you have interrupted and redirected your thoughts, the final step allows you to self-regulate, which means to create (or regain) your balance, as well as peace of mind, body, and spirit. First, do this simple breathing exercise: Breathe deeply into your tummy, using your diaphragm and not your upper chest. Hold that breath for three seconds and exhale slowly, counting backwards from three. Repeat three times until your heart rate relaxes and you feel okay. Now, engage your thoughts in such a way that generates awe, wonder, and gratitude. You can do this in any number of ways—the simplest one might be to continue to focus on your breath, but now start engaging fully in the thought of how miraculous breathing is. Feel gratitude for the clean air moving in and out of your lungs, filling you with life and energy. Even the wallpaper could be a focal point. Think about how many people had to be involved in the process of getting that paper on that wall. The designer, the marketer, the buyer, the manufacturer, the distributor, the laborer, and so on. Again, immerse yourself in this thought process to the point that you begin to feel a sense of awe and wonder about the complicated process of making something so seemingly simple.

In our scenario with the bridge, imagine you are focusing on the line in the road. You might start thinking about what a simple but extraordinary thing that is—a simple line that keeps thousands of drivers safely separated as they pass each other by. You might feel gratitude for the line, for the smoothness of the road, and for the miracle of engineering that is the bridge that allows you to safely cross the river without getting wet, just as tens of thousands of other drivers have done over the years. You could feel gratitude to the people who designed and built the bridge. You are regulating your emotions naturally, by thinking about something interesting and calming that evokes gratitude and wonderment. And remember, because thoughts are chemical, you just changed your brain chemistry!

Congratulations, you just used the I.R.S tools to stop a panic attack in its tracks! This is a process that is easy to learn and it's something you can do at anytime, in any place. The more you do this, the more natural it will become, until you will barely be conscious of going through the steps to Interrupt, Redirect, and Self-Regulate. But don't beat yourself up if it takes you some time to get accustomed to the process, and don't forget to forgive yourself for allowing these scary thoughts to dominate and direct your life experience in the first place. It's become so habitual to indulge in scary thoughts during anxious moments that you almost had no choice. Now you know that you have a choice. Choose to feel good about yourself. Choose to not scare yourself. Choose peace of mind.

GUIDED MEDITATION FOR SELF-REGULATION

This meditation is slightly different than the meditations in the previous chapters. The previous meditations were focused on supporting new thought concepts and altruistic perceptions about life for positive change. The focus of this meditation is to train the brain to respond with a purpose and a plan rather than simply react to an anxiety attack. This empowers you with a choice, and a process for managing an anxiety attack rather than it managing you.

To prepare for this meditation, find a quiet place without interruption.

Convince yourself that outside noises will not disturb you. Remind yourself that this guided meditation exercise is for your highest good.

Begin by tightening your muscles as tightly as you can. Tighten your face, neck, and shoulders, and hold it. Now, tighten your arms, fingers, legs, and toes. Hold it. Now release—release completely. Allow your body to be limp and relaxed.

Take a moment here and if you choose, invite your spiritual guides, your God, or your angels to join you on this relaxation journey.

Now, take a deep breath into the fullness of your lungs.

And exhale, releasing all of the stress from your mind, body, and spirit.

Breathe in again deeply, the air of confidence and surety.

Breathe out fear and doubt.

Breathe in the air of peace and tranquility.

Breathe out all controlled thought.

Now, being conscious of your mental and physical state of relaxation, on the count of three you will double your relaxed state

One. Two. Three.

You are now walking through a safe and peaceful field on a warm spring day toward a beautiful pond.

You can feel the soft, moist green grass beneath your feet.

Feel the warmth of the sun on your shoulders and your face.

You can hear the rustle of the leaves on the trees, and feel the gentle breeze moving through your hair.

As you approach the pond, find a perfect place to sit by the water's edge.

Notice that beside you is a soft, round pebble.

Reach for it and effortlessly toss it into the water.

Notice the ripples in the water from the entrance of the pebble. They grow in size and number then begin to disappear into the edges of the pond.

Now look beneath the water. Your pebble is reaching the sandy floor of the pond. As the pebble comes to rest, millions of tiny sand particles ascend in unison and then each and every one of them begins to descend, encircling and finally resting alongside your pebble.

As your pebble is at rest, so too are you at rest.

Breathe and rest.

Breathe and rest with your newfound skills for thought management: Interrupt, Redirect, and Self-regulate.

These are your IRS tools for positive mental management, peace of mind being your declared primary goal.

Make these words your own words:

I have a clear intention of what I want my thought-life to be.

The quality of my life is a mirror image of the contents of my thoughts.

Viewing my world and experiencing my life through a peaceful, serene mind, is my desire.

It is what I want to create for myself.

My mind can conceive peace; my mind can achieve peace.

With my IRS tools I have better control over the contents of my thoughts.

When undesirable thoughts enter my mind I say, with authority, STOP! GET OUT!

My mind is a safe place and comforting place for me to be. I choose my thoughts, beginning, middle, and end, to please me.

Breathe. One. Two. Three.

I am at peace with the world; I am at peace with me; I am peace of mind.

Breathe. One. Two. Three.

I don't hesitate to demand that an unwanted thought exit immediately. Again, I say with conviction and authority, STOP! GET OUT!

My mind is a safe and comforting place for me to be. You are not welcome here. You are not in alignment with my goal to have peace of mind.

Breathe. One. Two. Three.

I am at peace with the world; I am at peace with me; I am peace of mind.

Breathe. One. Two. Three.

I have dominion over my thoughts. The content of my thoughts determines the quality of my life.

I no longer welcome scary, unrealistic, tragic thoughts to enter my mind.

When they slip in, I am always there in an instant to demand their immediate exit!

I say, with fierce determination, STOP! GET OUT!

My mind is a safe and comforting place for me to be. You cannot come in. GET OUT NOW!

Breathe. One. Two. Three.

I am at peace with the world; I am at peace with me; I am peace of mind.

Breathe. One. Two. Three.

I am no longer afraid of my thoughts. I am the gate-keeper of thoughts. I only allow thoughts in my mind that are for my highest good.

I use my I.R.S tools in a powerful positive way. I will Interrupt, Redirect, and Self-Regulate my body, mind, and spirit any and every time I need to.

I am the security guard over the content of my thoughts. Negative, self-defeating thoughts are unwelcome intruders and will be escorted OUT immediately.

I have the ability, strength, and courage to redirect my thoughts to those that are in alignment with my primary goal to have peace of mind.

I am able to imagine myself going about my day with a confident, peaceful mind, attracting positive energy to body, mind, and spirit.

I imagine success in all areas of my life. When I speak, I speak with the calm presence of a peaceful mind. When I walk, my stride is gentle but firm, sure of my direction and purpose.

I am getting better every day. I am feeling better each day, full of hope and dreams.

The quality of my life is improving each day as I increase the volume of positive, powerful thought-energy.

I am using my I.R.S. tools to accomplish my goal of peace of mind.

I am more self-confident, self-assured, and self-reliant every day in every way.

I am getting better and better everyday.

I love life.

I am participating in the joyful journey of life.

I am not a victim of life, I am an adventurous, creative, curious traveler on the journey of life.

I walk with composure, assurance, grace, and dignity. My positive thoughts create positive energy that radiates from my smile.

I'm not waiting for life to happen to me. I happen to life.

I am happy, joyous, and free.

I am peace of mind, every day in every way.

I love life. I love me.

When you are ready, you may emerge from your relaxed state, feeling better than you did before, knowing that you are richer in mind, body and spirit for having had this experience. And so you are.

CHAPTER TEN

Step 7:
Making Conscious Choices About Your Emotions

[T]he little emotions are the great captains
of our lives and we obey them without realizing it.
—Vincent Van Gogh, Letter to Theo (July 1889)

If you were throwing a dinner party, would you just throw open your door and leave it to chance who ended up sharing your table and your lovingly prepared meal? No, I didn't think so. But you might be surprised to learn that you do something similar each and every day, in a place even more intimate than your dining room.

I'm talking about your emotions. Have you ever considered consciously choosing which emotions you will entertain at the table of your heart and mind? I know I didn't. And neither did Vincent Van Gogh, according to his famous quote above. For many years, I was a reactionary puppet to my emotions. Whatever I was feeling, that's what I reacted to and I stayed with it for dear life. It's as if I were a slave to whatever emotion I happened to be feeling at any given moment. If I was happy, that was great—who hasn't wanted to ride the happy wave till the sun goes down? If I was angry, I stayed with that feeling until it consumed me, and continued on that script until it played itself out. Usually this meant I doled my anger out to several different (undeserving) people until the emotion subsided. If I was feeling self-pity, watch out. I would find my victim, hold him emotionally hostage, and dump my sick, sad story on him until we both wanted to crawl into a fetal position and cry.

To live in the negative emotions like anger and self-pity is not to live at all; it's to endure. Nor does it remotely resemble having peace of mind. If our emotional thoughts dictate the quality of our lives, as well as our physical health, and we are suffering, then we have to do something drastically different about our emotional states. Step 7 of the Escape Anxiety process will teach you how to get control of your emotions by learning how to make conscious choices between them. This is not as easy as it sounds, however, because first we have to be able to identify which emotions we are actually engaging in. Our emotions can be deceiving.

Naming Your Emotions

We typically classify our emotions in four very narrow categories: happy, glad, mad, and sad. This is a gross underrepresentation of our capacity to feel. We are also cheating ourselves of the full experience of having an emotion. For example, if I'm sitting on park bench enjoying watching a flock of geese playing in a beautiful pond with a lovely water fountain in the center, and I said that I was "happy," instead of acknowledging that I was experiencing a sense of awe and wonderment at the natural beauty I was witnessing at play, I would have muted my full experience of that event. Think about how vastly different those two explanations feel.

It's also important to take the time to really identify a negative emotion. Oftentimes we will feel angry and say that we're mad, but if we look at the situation with emotional honesty we can find that a deeper emotion is masking itself as anger. We might actually be embarrassed, intimidated, or ashamed. These are difficult to admit to at times, but until you identify what you're actually feeling or what feeling is fueling your feelings, you will have little hope of resolving it because you can't challenge it.

For example, if you are angry over your boss's negative comment about a task you completed, you might actually be feeling irritated and annoyed that he didn't make a positive comment on the task prior to this one, which fueled the fire of your more intense feeling now. If you had been able to identify your original feelings when your boss didn't acknowledge the good job you did on the first task, and were willing to be vulnerable and honest enough to express this with your boss at the time, you very likely wouldn't have had all that stored up resentment when the later event took place.

I had always prided myself on being an honest person, but when I realized how emotionally dishonest I could be with myself, I was stunned. I didn't purposefully do this. I just didn't have the awareness that I needed to look beneath the surface of my emotions. I also didn't have a very large vocabulary to reference in helping me to determine what I was really feeling. It is sort of like looking for paint for a wall in a room. You might think you know what color you like until you look at all the colors that are available. Then your options become very rich. When I began to look deeper, I had a much better understanding of myself and my true vulnerabilities. Here are just a few emotions to consider as you begin to learn more about yourself:

Happy, Relieved, Assured, Confident, Capable, Able, Excited, Enthusiastic, Joyful, Peaceful, Content, Exhilarated, Hopeful, Grieved, Agonized, Defeated, Miserable, Ignored, Exhausted, Disappointed, Disrespected, Miserable, Suspicious, Neglected, Hopeless, Sad, Crushed.

When our emotions, good or bad, get too high or too low we seek relief from the intensity or stress. In a nutshell, this is why all addictions are rooted in stress and anxiety. We seek relief from things that make us calm, relaxed, or bring us up and out. This could be food, sex, alcohol, drugs, shopping, gaming, gambling, and many other activities and chemicals that make us feel better, quicker.

Once you are comfortable with using the tools I have offered here, you will be able to better identify what emotions you are engaging in, and respond with a conscious choice.

The Tale of Two Wolves

One day during my years of working for Brighton Hospital in Brighton Michigan, I was preparing for a lecture with the patients. I started fumbling through old files that were packed full of psychological inspirations that were great for building a lecture. One file was full of Native American quotes and teachings for spiritual and emotional healing. I came across a profound Old Cherokee legend, and it was again one of those light-bulb moments. Never could I, or anyone I knew, explain the nature of human emotions any clearer than this timeless tale.

It goes something like this:

> An old Cherokee chief was teaching his grandson a lesson about life.
>
> "A fight is going on inside me," he said to the boy. "It is a terrible fight and it is between two wolves.
>
> "One is evil—he is anger, envy, sorrow, regret, greed, arrogance, self-pity, guilt, resentment, inferiority, lies, false pride, superiority, self-doubt, and ego.
>
> "The other is good—he is joy, peace, love, hope, serenity, humility, kindness, benevolence, empathy, generosity, truth, compassion, and faith.
>
> "This same fight is going on inside you—and inside every other person, too."
>
> The grandson thought about it for a minute and then asked his grandfather, "Which wolf will win?"
>
> The old chief simply replied, "The one you feed."[37]

An Invitation to Dine

Let's examine this legend more closely, going back to the metaphor of your dinner party. Let's say that emotions are people, and Mr. Judgment came knocking on the door looking for you to feed him a delicious meal that you spent a lot of time preparing. You ask yourself, "Is this someone I want in my home, to share an intimate dining experience with? Do I want to get to know Mr. Judgment better? Do I really want to feed him my lovingly prepared food?" Remember, you have a choice.

What about when Ms. Pity comes knocking at the door? She is greedy, and always takes more than she should, and then tries to justify her selfishness with all her sad stories. And, when the dinner is over, she leaves you feeling empty and hopeless. Is this someone you really want to feed and spend your time with? Remember, you have a choice; you are in control. It's your dining table and you hold the keys to the door. Ah, look who just popped in, Mr. Jealousy. Well, well, it's been a while since you've seen him. You're reminded of how piercingly deceptive his voice can be and how much internal strife you feel when he visits. There is always the aftermath of wreckage you have to clean up with your loved ones every time you believe his stories as truth. Quick—show him to the door!

You hear the doorbell again. Oh, thank goodness, it's Hope! Quick, invite her in to sit with you. You've been waiting for her. You thought she was going to stand you up! But here she is. "Please sit," you invite her, "What can I get for you to eat and eat and eat? I hope you brought an overnight bag, I'd like for you to stay a while. I always feel bright when you're here. I smile more and for some reason I begin to think about fun things I can do for myself and others."

You know that all of the emotions, good and bad, are going to come knocking. You can't get rid of them altogether—they are part of the human condition and sometimes even necessary. But the quality of your life depends on how much time, effort, and energy you choose to give each of them. You have a choice over how much attention each one gets. The dinner party scenario is designed to heighten your awareness of your choice over your emotions. When we're talking about thoughts and emotions being chemical, this is not a small matter. You need to protect your mind with as much diligence as you protect your home. If you are interested in increasing the quality of your life and your emotional health, you must give careful consideration to the emotions you choose to listen to, and give your time to. If you're at all like me, you won't ever look at emotions in the same way again. And that's a good thing.

EXERCISE: *Create Your Guest List of Emotions*

Take a look at all the emotional choices you have at any given moment. Which emotions have a seat at the dining table of your mind? If there are some you might choose to un-invite, those that are no longer welcome in the sacred space of your emotional house, write them down to remind you that they are not invited to your sacred dining experience. They serve no good purpose and are not helpful. Write them down so that when they show up they will not be on your guest list and can be promptly shown the door.

Now, write down all the emotions you want to invite. These are the emotions that are in alignment with your declared purpose to have, hold, and maintain peace of mind. They are helpful and will enhance your dining experience in a multitude of ways. Write down your guest list and they will all gladly come to your sacred dining experience.

GUIDED MEDITATION FOR MAKING CONSCIOUS CHOICES ABOUT YOUR EMOTIONS

Now, you are ready for this guided meditation, designed to heighten your awareness of your power over your emotions, which incorporates the beautiful Two Wolves legend.

To prepare for this meditation, find a quiet place without interruption.

Convince yourself that outside noises will not disturb you. Remind yourself that this guided meditation exercise is for your highest good.

Begin by tightening your muscles as tightly as you can. Tighten your face, neck, and shoulders, and hold it. Now, tighten your arms, fingers, legs, and toes. Hold it. Now release—release completely. Allow your body to be limp and relaxed.

Take a moment here and if you choose, invite your spiritual guides, your God, or your angels to join you on this relaxation journey.

Now, take a deep breath into the fullness of your lungs.

And exhale, releasing all of the stress from your mind, body, and spirit.

Breathe in again deeply, the air of confidence and surety.

Breathe out fear and doubt.

Breathe in the air of peace and tranquility.

Breathe out all controlled thought.

Now, being conscious of your mental and physical state of relaxation, on the count of three you will double your relaxed state.

One. Two. Three.

You now find yourself walking in a beautiful valley, in a field of green.

The grass beneath your feet is soft and moist. You are safe and secure and at complete peace on your journey through the field toward the base of a small mountain.

You are comforted by the bird songs you hear in the distance.

It is a fresh fall morning. The trees greet you with a beautiful display of rich colors.

You are awed by nature's impeccable timing and flare for dramatics as it introduces and escorts in yet another beautiful new season.

The air is warmed by the sun's luminous rays. You are comforted by the soft breeze brushing against your skin.

You have reached the base of the small mountain and have found the path that has been cleared for your journey.

You have come here today willing to climb to higher places for higher learning. You are happy to be here, ready and eager to reach the gifts that await.

Your climb is surprisingly easy—it is almost as if you are floating.

Your breath is easy; your steps are sure.

Having tapped into your adventurous soul, amazed by your tenacious and courageous spirit, you move farther and farther up the mountain, each step fueled with more energy and curiosity than the one before.

Step, reach, and breathe.

Step, reach, and breathe.

You have come a long way and have found the top of the mountain. There is a perfect clearing and a soft, safe place to rest.

Sit, rest, breathe, and absorb.

Remember the wise tale the Cherokee grandfather told his beloved grandson.

"A fight is going on inside me," he says to the boy. "It is a terrible fight and it is between two wolves. One is evil—he is anger, envy, sorrow, regret, greed, arrogance, self-pity, guilt, resentment, lies, false pride, superiority, self-doubt, and ego. The other wolf is a good wolf—he is joy, peace, love, hope, serenity, humility, kindness, benevolence, empathy, generosity, truth, compassion, and faith."

The grandfather says to the grandson, "This same fight is going on inside you—and inside every other person, too."

The grandson thinks about it for a minute and then asks his grandfather, "Which wolf will win?"

The old chief simply replies, "The one you feed."

From the wise man's story, imagine yourself setting a table with your favorite dishes, each dish rich in nutrients, flavor, and color—mouthwatering, irresistible temptations.

The food is divine; space at the table is limited; your time is precious.

You are hungry to nourish your body, mind, and spirit with an intimate dining experience. You must carefully choose your dining companions, as each emotion from the good and evil wolf are possible companions.

Who is it that you wish to nourish and help grow in strength, endurance, and power?

You must choose. Will it be the stalking lioness of anger and resentment, or will it be the soaring eagle of truth and compassion?

Who is that you wish to nourish and help grow in strength, endurance, and power? Will it be the voracious vulture of envy, greed, and false pride? Or will it be the cuddly koala bear of peace, love, and hope?

The guests you choose to feed will dine with you, sharing your nutrients, your space and your time.

The guests that you choose to feed will grow in strength, presence, and power—with you and over you. Today you are keenly aware of the emotional wolves you choose to feed.

Knock as they may, you have choice over whom you allow to enter, stay, and join to feast with you at the dining table of your mind.

Your emotional dining choices mirror the quality of your life.

Today, the emotions you choose to feed will be in agreement with your commitment to have, own, and hold peace of mind.

You will choose to feed, nourish, and dine with love, hope, joy, and compassion. You will pass the bread to empathy, generosity, and compassion. Serenity, humility, and kindness always have a seat at the dining table of your mind.

These are the gentle emotional creatures you choose to feed and sustain in strength, power, and presence in your life.

You are getting stronger and healthier every day in every way.

Enjoy your meal with love, hope and joy. Watch as they grow in strength, power, and presence.

The bellies of serenity, humility, and kindness are fat and happy.

Empathy, generosity, and compassion are bursting with energy from their nutritious meal, eager to give of themselves in gratitude for the delicious meal and pleasure of your company.

You are growing stronger every day in every way by the wise choices you make and your diligence in holding true to your commitment to have and to own your own peace of mind.

You have complete control over your thoughts, emotions, actions, and reactions.

The positive mental attitudes and emotions you choose benefit you in powerful, positive ways.

You are feeling stronger today than any other day, getting better and better each day in every way with each powerful, positive choice you make.

Breathe and rest in the power of your positive choices.

When you are ready, you may emerge from your relaxed state, feeling better than you did before, knowing that you are richer in mind, body, and spirit for having had this experience. And so you are.

CHAPTER ELEVEN

Step 8:
Rewriting Your Internal Dialogue

For as he thinketh in his heart, so is he.
—Proverbs 23:7

You know that little voice in your head—the one that keeps up a running commentary throughout everything you do? Also known as the "committee"? Yes, I mean the one that's always criticizing, predicting the worst, and then saying, "I told you so!" The conversation you have with yourself, about yourself. I'm sure you already know that that voice tends to make you feel bad, left to its own devices. But as we now understand, that little voice can actually alter your body chemistry.

In earlier chapters I demonstrated various ways in which thoughts and emotions can affect our brains and our bodies. This chapter will emphasize the strong impact of what we tell ourselves about ourselves—not only on our self-esteem, but on our brain chemistry. Step 8 in the Escape Anxiety program shows you how to rewrite that inner dialogue so that it no longer triggers self-destructive, anxious, toxic thought-chemicals to be released into your brain and body.

I find it helpful to think of thoughts as behaviors. How are your thoughts behaving lately? Are your thoughts saying nice, kind, and loving things to you throughout the day? "Carolyn, you are a strong, beautiful, worthy woman of the world." "James, you are a smart, compassionate, honorable man." Everyone's doing that, right?

Okay, maybe not. Unfortunately, most of our inner dialogue starts with "I can't," "I'm not," "I haven't," "I wish I was/would/could," or "I should . . . " Right? Well, don't "should" on yourself so much! We all know this isn't healthy for us, but we do it anyway. Negative "self-talk," as it's often called, is a thought behavior that is habitual and resistant to change. Not only does this cause our brains to release stress hormones, but we believe the things we tell ourselves about ourselves, reinforcing our old thought myths and feeding disorders like anxiety. Negative self-talk and thinking are all derived from that four-letter word *fear*. Fear-based thoughts, as discussed throughout this book, trigger those powerful chemicals called stress hormones to be released from the brain to the central nervous system—which is why much has been written on the theme of "change your thoughts, change your life."

Tips for Shifting Your Self-Talk

There is a quick, easy exercise to illustrate this. Pick a negative thought about yourself. Close your eyes and imagine saying it to yourself. Be aware of how it makes you feel. Stay with it until you feel it through your entire body. Now, take a few deep breaths and cleanse your thoughts. Try the same thing with a positive message. Feel the difference? Now, consider the compound effect.

Here's another quick exercise to demonstrate this. Pick up a glass of water and hold it in one hand out to the side of your body, without resting your arm on anything. Just hold the glass with your hand in the air. Now, think about how much it weighs. Most people will guess a regular eight-ounce glass weighs somewhere around a pound. Keep holding the glass. You will quickly realize that the longer you hold that glass the heavier it feels. This is what it feels like to the mind/body when we hold a negative thought about ourselves. It quickly gets very heavy indeed! Negative thoughts weigh us down.

Here's another mental exercise you can do to better understand the idea that your thoughts are chemical. Imagine you're standing at a soda fountain and your cup represents your brain. What are you having today? A little self-doubt soda with a splash of self-deprecating sugar-free tea? Or will you have a little self-confidence punch with a squirt of love-yourself limeade? You get to decide—with every thought you tell yourself about yourself. Just remember, there are very real physical consequences to your choice.

Okay, everyone, so just think good thoughts about yourself and all will be well and fine. Goodnight. Ah, if only it were that easy! Unfortunately, as we've already seen, changing these deep-rooted patterns is not a simple matter—especially those patterns that relate to how we see ourselves. We've each spent a lifetime developing our thought behaviors as the result of our experiences, both positive and negative. The positive ones are not usually a problem, but the negative ones trip us up, time and time again. For example, most of us decided something about ourselves as a result of our first shame experience, as we discussed in chapter seven. Let's take a look at how these thoughts are created in the deepest part of our minds and why they are so resistant to change.

Our impulse to negatively self-talk goes back to our perfectionist tendencies. Each time we believe we fall short of perfection, we give ourselves an internal tongue-lashing. Remember that our subconscious mind can't distinguish between real or imagined threats or negativity. Our bodies respond according to the information we feed them. If we are constantly down on ourselves, doesn't it stand to reason that we would feel sad? Of course it does.

The shame factor related to anxiety is a perfect seed that grows into this pattern of constant tongue-lashings. When you have a panic attack, it's like being betrayed by your body. You were busy presenting your "I've got it all together" mask to the world, and then, *bam!* Your body messed it up. If you've had this experience, you know exactly how that internal relationship becomes very verbally abusive. It's really not that different than when someone you know very well embarrasses you in front of an important client or peer. You would not have kind words to say to that person after such an incident.

Another common way these abusive internal dialogues start is in early childhood, based on things said to us by others, often parents or siblings. Some examples of messages that I've heard from my clinical chair are: "You're just like your loser of a father;" "You stupid idiot, what were you thinking;" "You're fat—nobody will ever want to marry you;" and on and on. Sadly, these messages are adopted and become our own internal dialogue. We need to divorce this kind of thought behavior!

One of biggest challenges in changing the tone of our self-talk is learning to recognize when it's happening. For most of us, negative self-talk happens so naturally and with such frequency that we often don't consciously realize we are doing it. Here's one simple tip, and I mean simple: When you wake up each day, decide that you're going to reserve a particular time during the day to beat yourself up about whatever you feel the urge to beat yourself up about. Maybe you've procrastinated on something, eaten something you said you weren't going to eat, or behaved in an unpleasant way toward someone you love. Whatever it is, decide that you're going to endure the negative self-talk beating at 6:00 p.m. for fifteen minutes. You can even set your alarm to remind you to do it. Sounds silly doesn't it? But it works, and I'll tell you why. When you make a conscious decision to change a behavior, you become more aware of the behavior you've decided to change. During the day, you will more easily catch yourself making unkind remarks to yourself.

Secondly, I really want you to spend that fifteen minutes giving yourself that tongue-lashing you decided you had coming. What you will most likely find is that you'll begin to defend yourself against yourself. For example: You might be mad at yourself about eating something you had said you weren't going to eat. While you're beating yourself up about it, you'll find another side of you speaking up. It might say something like, "Well I'm just not ready to give it up yet." Or, "I'll try harder tomorrow." Or maybe "I'll ask for help." This happens because now you are consciously talking to yourself instead of subconsciously being a victim of an unbridled voice that has no "off" button!

As a therapist who hears the innermost secret thoughts of other human beings as part of my job, I can't tell you how often I feel deep pain for patients who just bully themselves relentlessly. It brings to mind the old saying "with friends like that, who needs enemies?" One of my patients, Lydia, used to constantly beat herself up about her smoking. She had overcome her addiction to alcohol but was not yet able to overcome her addiction to nicotine. Interestingly, she was smoking only about three cigarettes a day, at the most, and sometimes didn't have one at all, which is extremely rare for a nicotine addict (and in this case I use the term addict lightly).

But that was unacceptable to her. She would go into deep states of depression about her failures and just beat the crap out of herself. It was painful to witness. Lydia had chosen to focus on that aspect of herself for the vast majority of the day and completely neglected the fact that she had overcome her addiction to alcohol, which was a huge accomplishment, or the fact that she was a dedicated and active mother to her children, a great wife to her husband, and was adored by her community. She made an unfortunate choice to feed the source of her pain instead of the source of hope and gratitude for her progress.

Let me remind you again that most thought behaviors have some positive purpose. It's when they get out of control that they have a negative impact on the quality of our lives. With respect to self-criticism, it's important to realize that pain is the great motivator to change. So you have to determine if your negative self-talk is trying to get you to change something or if it's trying to tear away the layers of self-esteem. And even if it is trying to change something, if you're just not ready to make that change, it's important to accept yourself and stop self-criticizing. Otherwise you are putting yourself at risk of having two serious problems rather than one. Feeding this kind of pain will lead to anxiety and depression. This is exactly what happened to Lydia. Her anxiety and depression progressed as her addiction to nicotine stayed the same. Now she had two very real issues, making it even harder for her to conquer her original issues because she was so defeated mentally and emotionally by her relentless self-abuse.

If you're struggling with something you want to change, I suggest you make a decision each morning as to whether or not today is the day to change. If it's not, try to let it go until that magical 6:00 p.m. verbal lashing appointment with yourself. If it is the day to change and you fail, acknowledge your progress and search for other ways to accomplish your goals, like asking for help and support from others who are struggling with the same situation. Change of any kind is hard, so don't make it harder by being hard on yourself.

Another great way to become more aware of what you are telling yourself is to try the following simple exercise for just a day. Put a handful of pennies in your right pocket. Each time you think something negative about yourself, switch a penny from your right to your left pocket. At the end of the day, you should have a pretty good idea how much you're investing in negative self-talk.

Positive Self-Talk

Your words have power, whether they are spoken or thought. This is true for both positive and negative sentiments. So once you start to get a handle on your negative self-talk, you need to also start cultivating the habit of positive self-talk. Remember, the goal is not to be perfect, whatever that would mean, but to shift the balance from mostly negative to mostly positive. Let's say your current state of mind is 80 percent negative self-talk and 20 percent positive self-talk. You can estimate this, or use a version of the pie chart exercise we did in chapter eight to measure approximate percentages. A reasonable goal for you might be to shift to 80 percent positive self-talk and 20 percent negative. It's not perfect, but for most that would be a life-altering shift.

Let me warn you that positive self-talk can be a double-edged sword. In most cases, if we affirm to ourselves our positive attributes, we will feel better. However, if we affirm positive attributes that we don't really believe to be true, we can actually end up feeling worse about ourselves and in turn create another cycle of negative, self-defeating dialogue. So if you're engaging in positive self-talk, it's important to do so in such a way that deeply internalizes the positive beliefs, rather than just giving voice to them.

As we've seen, meditation is one of the best ways to internalize positive reinforcement messages. When it comes to changing internal dialogue, I think it's important to come up with a mantra—a short, memorable phrase you can repeat to yourself regularly, not just in times of stress but throughout your day. Deepak Chopra explains that the word *mantra* in Sanskrit comes from *man*, which is the root of the word for mind, and *tra*, which is the root of the word instrument. "A mantra is therefore an instrument of the mind," he writes, "a powerful sound or vibration that you can use to enter a deep state of meditation."[38] I'll share with you my mantra and tell you the backstory for each word. My mantra is:

I am a capable, able, creative, loving child of God.

I use the word *capable* because often the voice in my head tells me I'm not smart enough, educated enough, or motivated enough to do anything extraordinary. But when I say that I am capable, it reminds me that I do have great knowledge in some areas, I am educated in my field of work, and I exhibit the ability to be motivated in other things I've accomplished, like running a half marathon. Although I struggle with believing I am capable, I am able to resolve the internal conflict and come to the belief that I actually am capable of doing what I want to do.

I use the word *able* to remind me that although at times I feel shortchanged in my life by not having the money or natural talents or support that other more successful people have, it is true that I have overcome many challenges in my life; I am a strong woman and I have many gifts that I can even improve on if I'm willing to put forth the effort. Here, again, I struggle with self-pity and lack of confidence but when I take a really good look at who I am and what I've accomplished in my life I can resolve this conflict too and come to believe that I am indeed able to do things in life that bring me happiness and a sense of purpose.

I use the word *creative* because sometimes my mind tells me I'm dumb and dull and I always fall short of perfection and I'm not as good as whomever I happen to be comparing myself to that day. But if I challenge that message, I realize that I am pretty creative. I'm solution-oriented. I have created interesting, helpful, and valuable things in my life, like my meditations as well as my sense of style in clothes and home décor. Yes, I am in fact a creative creature when I think about it, and I can accept that about myself.

I use *loving* because it reminds me that I love many people in my life and many love me too. I like that about myself. And finally, I use *child of God* to reinforce to myself that I am not God, and I am not supposed to have all the answers. I am not supposed to have infinite knowledge and wisdom. In fact, in the bigger picture I am just a child, growing and learning like all the other children of all ages on Earth. I am going to make mistakes and I am going to be humbled by my mistakes and someone or something is going to give me grace. How do I know this? Because it has always been that way. That's who I am. And it's not only okay to be me—I'm a capable, able, creative, loving child of God!

I have found that a good time to repeat my mantra to myself is when I'm exercising or walking a fair distance. It gives me focus and I can make it harmonious with my steps. It also gives me time to reflect on the true meaning of each of those words. They are not just words to me, as you can see. Each of them has a special meaning and affirmation.

EXERCISE: Create Your Own Mantra

Here is an exercise to help you create your own mantra.

1. Write down the most important goal you want to accomplish, short-term or long-term in your life.

   For example, you might want to increase your self-esteem, or you may want to accomplish something more specific like getting in shape, running a marathon, learning a new language, or going back to school. Whatever you choose, it should be something you want for yourself, not for others.

2. Write down all the reasons why you are capable of accomplishing this goal.

   Think back at previous accomplishments in your life and pull truths from them. For example, I did really well in school, so I know I'm an achiever. Or, I may be out of shape now, but I was once a competitive tennis player. I know I'm dedicated and can achieve what I set my mind to. I can, I did, I am able. Write down whatever it is that feels good to you and that you truly believe about yourself, based on your history.

3. Write down something about yourself that represents your spiritual nature.

   This might be something like: I'm humble, I'm generous, I'm thoughtful, I'm loving, I'm a mentor, I'm a helper, I'm a spiritual being. Whatever feels like your best spiritual attribute.

4. Make a sentence using three of the reasons why you're capable of achieving your goal and at least one of your spiritual gifts.

5. Make it short and sweet so you can remember it easily and it can have impact when you say it. Good luck with developing your personal mantra! Just know that you can change it at any time, but it's good to become so familiar with it that it is second nature to you and ready to roll off your tongue at any moment.

EXERCISE: Turn Your Trauma Time Line into an Achievement Time Line

The final exercise in this chapter is an extension to the one in chapter two where you created your trauma time line. Now is the time to create a powerful balance with your trauma time line by adding to it your achievement time line.

Simply use the bottom part of your trauma time line from chapter two and add your achievements. Follow the same time frame markings and measurement of impact your personal achievements have had on your life. I emphasize *on your life* because these personal achievements may not have meant anything to anyone else but you, and that is all that matters!

Below is my Achievement Time Line, for you to get an idea of how to create your own.

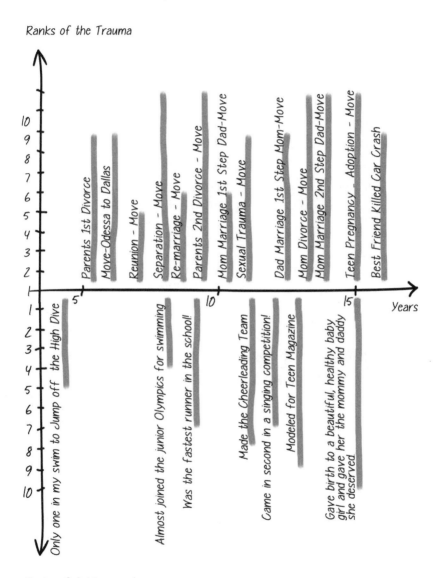

Ranks of the Trauma

Ranks of Achievements

Suzanne's Achievement Time Line

Once you've created your Achievement Time Line, I encourage you to look at both of your time lines and honor the fact that the person you are now is a balance of both the negative things that happened to you and the positive choices you've manifested in your life. This *is* life; it ebbs and flows, with ups and downs.

As odd as this may sound, I can tell you that I'm truly grateful for the pain and suffering I have encountered in my life. Let me make the distinction between gratitude and happiness. I'm not happy about my suffering, but I am grateful for it. I'm grateful because it has been my suffering that has shaped my deepest spiritual gifts and motivated me to accomplish things I would have never imagined. It's not about what happens to us, it's about what we choose to do about it. Now, let's make some lemonade—after we meditate.

GUIDED MEDITATION FOR REWRITING YOUR INTERNAL DIALOGUE

This final meditation will support you in moving into each day knowing that you are never alone. You are the answer, you are the key, you are your own best friend.

To prepare for this meditation, find a quiet place without interruption.

Convince yourself that outside noises will not disturb you. Remind yourself that this guided meditation exercise is for your highest good.

Begin by tightening your muscles as tightly as you can. Tighten your face, neck, and shoulders, and hold it. Now, tighten your arms, fingers, legs, and toes. Hold it. Now release—release completely. Allow your body to be limp and relaxed.

Take a moment here and if you choose, invite your spiritual guides, your God, or your angels to join you on this relaxation journey.

Now, take a deep breath into the fullness of your lungs.

And exhale, releasing all of the stress from your mind, body, and spirit.

Breathe in again deeply, the air of confidence and surety.

Breathe out fear and doubt.

Breathe in the air of peace and tranquility.

Breathe out all controlled thought.

Now, being conscious of your mental and physical state of relaxation, on the count of three you will double your relaxed state.

One. Two. Three.

You are walking to a quiet, beautiful, and safe place by the ocean's edge.

You can feel the grains of warm, moist sand beneath your feet.

You can feel the warmth of the sun on your shoulders and on your face.

You can feel the soft, subtle movement of the wind against your skin and through our hair.

You can hear the soft chatter of sea gulls in the distance.

You can see and hear the majesty of the movement of the ocean's water, which is home to another world of our creator's great creations.

You are warm; you are safe; you are amazed, curious and fascinated by the world around you—delighted to be a spectator and a participant.

As you walk along the sandy beach, you find a soft, clean blanket that has been prepared as your place of rest.

Find a comfortable position to rest on your blanket.

You have found your place of rest.

Now, breathe and rest.

Breathe in fresh pure air and a peaceful mind.

Exhale and rest.

The calls of the wild birds have faded.

You are at rest

Breathe and rest.

Make these words your own:

I am who I say I am.

Who I say I am is who I set out to be.

If I say that I am that, then that is what I work to prove myself to be.

When I say that I am the other, then that I what I give my energy and intention to be.

I work to make myself right about what I say that I am.

What I say that I am, is what I give power to.

What I say that I am has power.

My thoughts become words, my words become actions, my actions become habits, my habits become my character.

My thoughts become words, my words become actions, my actions become habits, my habits become my character.

I will no longer say, in my mind or aloud, things about me that I don't want to be true.

I will no longer give my power or intention to creating that which I do not truly desire to be.

I will give all my energy and power to the me that I long to be.

My thoughts and my words have power. I have choice over which words I choose to give power to.

I will define me in only positive terms.

I have a clear intention to be the very best me.

My thoughts and words reflect my desire to be the very best me.

I am confident, capable, and able.

I am fun, funny, and fabulous.

I am calm, compassionate, and caring

I am happy, joyous, and free.

I am intelligent, ethical, and entertaining.

I am wise, full of wonder, and wonderful.

I am resilient, tenacious, and determined.

I am a marvelous, miraculous creation.

I am courageous, composed, and quality.

I am love, loving, and beloved.

I am worthy of all that is good.

I am all that I need to be.

I am all that I choose to be.

I am because I chose to be.

I am happy, joyous, and free.

I am

Peace of mind.

When you are ready, you may emerge from your relaxed state, feeling better than you did before, knowing that you are richer in mind, body, and spirit for having had this experience. And so you are.

It's in the Cans

Success comes in "cans," not in "cannots."
A favorite maxim

Remember where we began my story—standing at the pantry in my kitchen, paralyzed by panic? In that desperate attempt to hold on to my last threads of sanity, I did what felt like a most insane thing. Reaching for the vegetable cans, I read those labels, one by one, desperately holding on to each word and searching my mind for its meaning and applications. I mean, seriously, what sane adult with a relatively high I.Q. has an internal conversation with herself about green beans and corn? No one! Yet what I've come to understand is that what I thought was a sign of further deterioration of my mind was in fact my first taste of the solution—the solution that would grow into this book. Reading those food cans was an instinctive act of self-regulation using a form of mindfulness meditation (although at that time in my life, I had never even heard of such a thing.)

Unknowingly, I was distracting myself from the thoughts that were causing and escalating my anxiety by reading the labels. Then I went deeper into focus by contemplating what each word meant, what it meant to me, and what it meant for humanity. Then I took a step further, engaging my senses by visualizing the garden where green beans grew, and imagining what green beans and salt tasted like. Through this simple act, I was pulling myself deeper into the present by focusing on what was in front of me and engaging my senses with a non-threatening thought process. I didn't realize it, but I was causing a switch to flip in my limbic system from activation of my sympathetic nervous system (Stress Response) to my parasympathetic nervous system (Relaxation Response).

Unfortunately, I was too late to prevent my hospitalization, and all the chaos that created in my life. My hope is that this book has reached you in time to prevent, or slow down, the runaway mind-train of anxiety in your life.

I've always loved the saying "success comes in 'cans,' not in 'cannots.'" Ironically, the secret to my successful recovery literally did come in those cans of food, although I wouldn't know it until much later. My understanding of this phrase took on a deeper meaning during my recovery, when I joined Alcoholics Anonymous and learned the famous "Serenity Prayer" by Reinhold Niebuhr, which the recovery movement has adopted as being so central to its work:

> *God, grant me the serenity to accept the things I cannot change,*
> *The courage to change the things I can,*
> *And the wisdom to know the difference.*

Success, I have come to understand, does not only lie in the cans. It also lies in the cannots—in recognizing and accepting, gracefully, those things that we cannot change so that we free up our energy for those things we can. I had unknowingly practiced this truth as well, that day as I stood in front of my kitchen pantry, when I surrendered to the realization that I could no longer cope with my disorder alone. Accepting this "cannot" was a critical step for me on my journey to emotional freedom. As you will have seen repeatedly as you did the exercises in this book, knowing your "cans" and your "cannots" is essential to mental health and stability.

I want to offer you my heartfelt thanks for joining me in the journey of this book, and allowing me to be your guide in understanding what anxiety is and learning the best practices for treating it and for sustainable recovery and management.

In closing, there are a few final words I want to share with you. I am in recovery from anxiety disorder, which means that my disorder is not active. I no longer have panic attacks, and in fact haven't had one since my hospitalization in 1991. I have, however, experienced symptoms of anxiety many times over the past twenty years, a few of which I have talked about in this book. I have always been able to identify the cause—whether it's something I've eaten; a chemical in an over-the-counter drug I may have taken; a medical condition like hypothyroidism, which I recently developed; the rapid buildup of lactic acid from my overzealous attempts to be an athlete; or my magical magnifying mind left to its own devices.

We, as anxiety sufferers, will always be charged with the responsibility of paying attention to these critical elements, including chemicals, health issues, and our thought life as we continue on our journey toward mental wellness. To help you in identifying possible triggers for your own anxiety, and making smart lifestyle choices to prevent future attacks, I've included the best information I can find on nutrition, chemicals, and exercise, as well as information about the dangers of substance abuse in the resources section at the end of this book. I'd encourage you to read through this carefully, and return to it as a reference whenever needed.

In fact, I hope you will return to all of the chapters in this book. It was not intended to be a one-time read. What I've learned in my quest to manage my mind is that perfectionism, resentments, control issues, and all the other factors we've discussed will pop up out of nowhere, it seems, at random times, giving me an opportunity to revisit my recovery skills and meditations. Keep this book handy for when those little critters surface in your life, as surely they will.

Please visit me online at EscapeAnxiety.com for more resources, inspiration, and ways to stay connected. My purpose is to teach, guide, and inspire peace of mind and passion for living in the face of adversity.

Thank you for letting me fulfill my life's purpose!

Please enjoy my personally recorded meditations with soothing, melodic background instrumentals that are included in my ESCAPE ANXIETY in-home therapeutic program at EscapeAnxiety.com

INFORMATION AND RESOURCES
FOR ANXIETY SUFFERERS

Nutrition for Peace of Mind

In chapter two we discussed the all the contributing components to anxiety and one of them was chemical use. Anxiety sufferers tend to be much more sensitive to some unsuspected chemicals and additives in food, drinks, and medication, which can exacerbate their symptoms and make it much more difficult for them to live a panic-free life, even with the proper medications.

As modern science and testing improves, researchers and scientists continue to find links between commonly consumed products and the exacerbation or even causation of anxiety disorders in children and adults. Keeping an eye out for these ingredients can reduce feelings of anxiety in non-sufferers and keep diagnosed anxiety=disorder patients feeling better. In this chapter I will be discussing some of the most common culprits for exacerbating anxiety that may be found in things you unknowingly consume regularly.

Sugar

Before the industrialization of the food world, processed sugars were rare and valuable commodities. With the advent of sugar processing technologies, sugar and sugar products became more and more accessible, and by 1830 the average American consumed 11 pounds of sugar per year. While that number may seem disturbing on its own, the average American consumed 155 pounds of sugar in the year 2000, and these numbers have continued to rise steadily since then.

Human bodies did not evolve to digest processed sugar, and the commonly known consequences of eating too much sugar—diabetes, obesity, and tooth rot, to name a few—are just the tip of the iceberg. Because the body has been tuned to process complex carbohydrates over years of evolutionary adaptation, simple carbohydrates and sugary snacks blast through the process of digestion and are absorbed quickly into the body. This phenomenon leads to a brief period of energy commonly known as a "sugar rush," which continues until the body falls into a sluggish state. Most people that experience this post sugar rush fallout, reach for a cup of caffeinated coffee or soda—which is, of course, also a problem for the anxiety sufferer.

Here's another example of how our bodies process sugar. Imagine that your body is a fireplace that has been designed to efficiently burn lumber. The consumption of complex, minimally processed foods is equivalent to putting another log on the fire, while eating foods high in processed sugars is akin to pouring lighter fluid directly onto the coals. Logs burn slowly, and keep the fire going for longer, while the lighter fluid burns brightly and then dies down quickly, leaving a charred, empty fireplace behind.

To make matters worse, the body's natural reaction to influxes of sugar is to increase insulin production, which naturally helps to reduce the level of sugar in the blood. When the initial sugar rush is gone, however, the insulin remains, and continues to lower the amount of sugar in the blood, potentially even lower than it was before the sugar was introduced. If we return to our fireplace metaphor, imagine that someone saw that your fire was burning too high, and came over with a bucket of water to douse the flames. Now the fireplace is soaked, and rekindling even the smallest fire will be even harder.

Drops and fluctuations in blood sugar level are known to activate stress responses in humans. Thousands of years ago, this alerted our ancestors' bodies to the urgency of their hunger, and would give them the motivating panic needed to find food. In today's sugar-rich environment, the sudden peaks and lows in blood sugar level trigger can trigger a biological panic reaction. These types of reactions have nothing to do with thought. You can be doing your very best work in managing your emotions and thoughts life and this could very well trump your efforts and cause a panic attack.

Additionally, sugar highs can cause blurred vision, fatigue, and difficulty thinking, while sugar crashes can lead to shaking, lethargy, and tension. For individuals who suffer from panic attacks or other anxiety, these feelings can simulate the beginning of a panic attack, increasing worry and enhancing anxiety and may even lead to a full on panic attack. Beware of sugar!

Artificial Sweeteners

While sugar is a negative influence on anxiety, artificial substitutes are far more pervasive than their more-natural counterpart. Reports of mood swings and anxiety after consuming man-made sweeteners, such as high fructose corn syrup and aspartame, are abundant, and the numbers of these reports continue to increase. Science still doesn't know the full scope of the impact sweeteners may have on mental health, but the science behind the toxicity of these substances is well known.

Because Aspartame, the most common sugar-free sweetener, is entirely synthetic, the human body has no pre-written process for digesting it. The small intestine makes its best attempt to break the bonds that bind together the molecule, and eventually manages to separate it into several substances—mainly phenylalanine, aspartic acid, and methyl alcohol. Because the body has difficulty recognizing these chemicals immediately, they are allowed to roam freely throughout the body, which can cause a host of immediate health problems such as dizziness, headaches, confusion, or even seizures.

Phenylalanine, the most common component in Aspartame, is converted into norepinephrine, and epinephrine, commonly known as adrenaline, by the body. These chemicals are normally released by the body as a response to stressful situations, and aim to prepare the body for fight or flight situations by accelerating breathing and heart rate, increasing muscle twitch responses and blood flow, and heightening situational awareness. Even for people who do not suffer from anxiety, a sudden influx of these brain chemicals can lead to sensations of energy and nervousness, and even a mild panic attack. Clearly, for people who already suffer from anxiety, this will create an experience of increased anxiety and disturbing panic like physical symptoms.

Aspartic acid, the second biggest component of Aspartame, also functions as a brain chemical relating to brain activity and excitement. Low levels of aspartic acid can be found in patients with depression, while high levels have been noted in patients who suffer seizures and strokes.

If too many of any of these brain chemicals are present in the brain at once, they can also lead to excitotoxicity—the process by which nerve cells are so heavily stimulated that they shut down their chemical receptors or die off completely. This mechanism is known to be involved in cases of ALS, Multiple Sclerosis, and Parkinson's disease, along with other neurodegenerative disorders, and can be highly detrimental to mental health and stability.

Salt

Unlike processed sugars and sweeteners, the human body is designed to handle regular salt intake. Our ancestors consumed an estimated 750 milligrams of salt per day, which is just around half of the daily dose that doctors recommend to modern patients. Sodium helps to maintain fluid balance and heart function, and the chloride ions that come bound to the sodium in table salt are processed into hydrochloric stomach acid, which is vital to digestive health. Sodium deficiency can actually result in brain swelling, heart failure, blood loss, or coma.

There is, however, a delicate balance that must be maintained when considering salt intake. Sodium overdose can be just as dangerous as sodium deficiency, depleting your body of potassium and increasing blood pressure. Potassium is responsible for regulating blood pressure, water retention, proper cell function, and muscle regulation, and low levels can lead to mental health issues such as depression, anxiety, and insomnia, and lead to other issues such as kidney stones, muscle spasms, headaches, and restless leg syndrome.

Anxiety patients who have been prescribed Lithium need to be especially careful with their salt levels, as salt can alter the effects of therapeutic lithium, disrupting the medical effects of the medication. Over-consumption of salt can strip lithium from the body, while sudden reduction in sodium levels, due to sweating, vomiting, diarrhea, or diet change, may result in lithium overdose and toxicity.

MSG

MSG, also known as monosodium glutamate or glutamic acid, is a common food additive that is derived from seaweed. It is highly prevalent in restaurants (particularly Chinese ones), frozen foods, and other processed goods in the United States, although it is more strictly regulated in other countries due to potential negative health effects. This additive is used in foods to enhance savory flavors, and can be used to reduce the amount of salt needed to achieve a desired level of salty flavor.

I personally was so relieved to when the word got out about the dangers of MSG. I would often leave a Chinese restaurant after a nice meal and feel an internal sense of unease that I couldn't pinpoint. It felt like a low level vibration throughout my body, coupled with an emotional hangover. You know that feeling of dull shame and regret after saying something you wish you hadn't? It was kind of like that.

What science has now found is that while small amounts of MSG are commonly considered to be safe for consumption, glutamic acid can be converted to neurotransmitters or active brain chemicals that can lead to excitotoxic effects similar to those produced by Aspartame. Although no studies have conclusively proven the negative effects of MSG, it has also been linked to neurodegenerative diseases such as ALS, Parkinson's, and Multiple Sclerosis, as well as negative symptoms such as tremors, hot and cold flashes, migraines, anxiety, panic attacks, and mood swings.

Many people have found themselves to be especially sensitive to MSG, reporting symptoms such as localized numbness or pressure, general weakness, heart palpitations, headaches, chest pain, nausea, and drowsiness. If you find yourself experiencing these symptoms after eating at a restaurant or consuming pre-processed foods, investigate if MSG might be the cause. You can also ask your waiter if the restaurant you're dining at uses MSG. This helps in avoiding the problem all together!

Food Dyes

I used to frequent a favorite Mexican restaurant for lunch, where I would often meet friends. Yet every time I left there, I felt a rise in my anxiety. This was long after my hospitalization and my anxiety was for the most part very under control, so you can imagine my angst when this would happen. I was using an artificial sweetener at the time, and thought maybe that was the culprit, so I quit using it. Still, I would leave that restaurant with anxiety. I couldn't figure it out. All I was eating were chips and salsa, and cheese enchiladas with red sauce, rice, and beans. I was baffled, until one day, driving home from work, I heard a reporter talk about the anxiety-inducing effects of red dye! Wow, I thought, that's it. There must be red dye in my enchilada sauce! I couldn't believe it. I wondered how many other people were experiencing the same thing and had absolutely no idea what was happening. I also wondered how many foods contained red dye. The answer to that is very disturbing.

Here's what we know. Earlier in our history, the food colorant industry was highly unregulated, and there were over 80 food dyes available for consumption. Modern testing methods and suspicions of these chemicals have resulted in the gradual banning of most of these dyes. Today, there remain only seven dyes that are approved for all food use, and two more that are restricted to specific uses such as the coloration of orange peels and hot dog or sausage casings.

Several of the dyes that remain in use in the United States have been banned already in other countries, such as Canada and Great Britain, due to suspected behavioral effects, especially in children. Testing is still ongoing to formalize the link between these chemicals and hyperactivity, anxiety, migraines, and cancer.

Red #40, also known as Allura red, my enchilada culprit, is the most common red colorant in America, and was originally created as a derivative of coal tar, although in most modern cases it is now derived from petroleum. It has been banned in Belgium, Denmark, France, Norway, Sweden, and Switzerland, although Norway and Sweden have since allowed it back into the market. Strong calls for the FDA to remove this dye from the market have been made since 2010, but food lobbies have kept it legal. You can find Red #40 in most red, pink, or orange colored beverages, processed fruits and meats, and in cold and cough medications, pill coatings, gums, and vitamins. Read your labels and ask your grocer and restaurant managers about their dye additives and write to your Governor to complain!

Yellow #5, also known as Tartrazine, is also a prime suspect in behavioral issues and psychological conditions in children. This chemical is also known to exacerbate asthma and prescription drug intolerance, and has been linked to cancer and chromosomal damage. This additive has been banned in Austria and Norway, and warnings against it have been issued all across the European Union. You can find Yellow #5 in Mountain Dew and other yellow sodas, yellow candies, many cheeses and macaroni and cheese kits, and canned fruits and pie fillings.

Aside from the effects that these chemicals can have on children, many adults also report mood swings and anxiety after consuming these and other artificial colorants. For anxiety sufferers who experience unexplained changes in brain function, cutting out or limiting synthetic dyes can greatly improve mental health and neurological stability.

Caffeine

Caffeine is the most commonly consumed psychoactive drug in the world, and it has become a social staple in most countries and cultures. Because it is found in such common beverages as coffee and tea, caffeine is rarely considered to be a drug by the average consumer, lawmaker, or physician, making it quite easily one of the most unregulated chemical stimulants consumed today.

Everyone is familiar with the more common positive effects of caffeine—improved focus and alertness and the feeling of being more awake—and recent studies have also shown some other potential health benefits. But for those who suffer from anxiety, the costs almost always outweigh the benefits. Not everyone, however, is as familiar with the various negative side effects of caffeine. These effects, some of which are presented with even the smallest dose of caffeine, include:

- Increased heartbeat
- Irregular heartbeat
- Elevated blood pressure
- Headaches

☙Decrease in serotonin levels

☙Nervousness

☙Depression

☙Irritability

☙Shakes or jitters

☙Sweating

☙Dehydration

☙Difficulty sleeping

Any of these symptoms alone can be dangerous, especially to a person who already suffers from an anxiety disorder, but the combination of these symptoms can increase worry and trigger panic attacks. Lack of sleep and low serotonin levels can cause or exacerbate the symptoms of depression and psychosis, and even the smallest amount of dehydration is known to cause depressive symptoms.

Caffeine-induced Anxiety Disorder is now a condition recognized by the Diagnostic and Statistical Manual of Mental Disorders, and other psychiatric disorders can be triggered, aggravated, or even simply mimicked by overuse of caffeine. If someone visited their doctor presenting any small few of the symptoms above, they might find themselves being treated for anxiety or depression without their caffeine intake ever being considered.

These effects may also not appear right away—caffeine users often find that they can drink significant amounts of caffeine for a long period of time, but will eventually reach a threshold where they suddenly begin suffering from neurological or psychological symptoms. Stimulants force the body into a hyper-vigilant state, pouring energy into preparing for a fight or flight reaction, and the human brain suffers from being in a constant state of simulated fear.

While millions of people simply start out their day with a cup of coffee, or enjoy a cup of tea in the afternoon, there are millions more who have begun to feel that they *need* caffeine to survive. As sugary coffee drinks become the social go-to, and caffeine-laden energy drinks rise in popularity among the youth, this dangerous stimulant slips in to our lives and starts to put down dangerous roots.

The caffeine lifestyle can increase intake of other toxic or dangerous trigger chemicals. Popular processed beverages that contain caffeine, such as energy drinks and Starbucks beverages, can also contain large quantities of processed sugars or artificial sweeteners, and can sometimes include artificial colorants. These trendy beverages are cocktails of addictive and neurotoxic ingredients, and have become so ingrained into the lives of some people that they are unaware of the true rate of their caffeine, calorie, and sugar consumption.

Caffeine-related hospitalizations increased by roughly one thousand percent between 2005 and 2009, and this number will surely continue to rise. Quitting caffeine is a difficult process, and stopping caffeine intake abruptly can worsen depression and cause fatigue, irritability, and painful headaches for months after the last sip. Caffeine is also a substance that is psychologically habit-forming—drinking a cup of coffee is part of the morning routine, or grabbing an energy drink with friends is a ritual after school—and it can be more difficult to break these habits because they are associated with positive stimuli.

To begin the process of kicking your caffeine habit, find an acceptable, low-caffeine substitute for your beverage of choice, and work on tapering down from there. Commercially brewed coffee and energy drinks have the highest caffeine content, usually ranging from one hundred to three hundred milligrams of caffeine per eight ounces. Downsizing your drink order from twenty ounces to a more reasonable size or replacing your coffee with a cup of tea can also be a great way to begin to limit caffeine intake, and brewed tea is more often free of colorants and sweeteners.

When I was hospitalized, one of the first things I had to give up was caffeine. I was not a happy camper about this although what it allowed me to do was to have a better sense of what caffeine was actually doing to my body. As a result I didn't have a caffeinated drink for over seven years. I occasionally will have one cup of coffee in the morning. But on days where I may encounter something stressful, like a public talk or group therapy, I skip it and save myself the anxiety!

Simple Carbohydrates

Much in the same way that refined sugar is too-quickly consumed by the body, simple carbohydrates and natural sugars such as those found in fruit, milk, and other heavily-processed goods like bread, cake, and chocolate provide short term energy that is spent quickly and leaves you prone to depression, energy depletion, and anxiety.

The quick energy rush and fall that you gain from simple carbohydrates leaves your body yearning for more energy, which can cause cravings for more sugar, fatty foods, or caffeine, which can each do damage on their own, and will continue to leave your body feeling unfulfilled.

Complex carbohydrates such as whole grains, starchy vegetables, beans, and leafy greens provide vitamins, minerals, and fiber, and take longer for your body to process. These are thought to create a calming, relaxing effect as your body digests and releases serotonin. The slow release of the energy from these carbohydrates will keep your hunger sated for longer, and will keep your body moving at a smooth, steady pace.

Processed and Nutrient-Deficient Foods

There are many contributing factors to the overall mental impact of consuming processed foods. Depending on the type of food, manufactured and pre-prepared foods can contain any of the above-listed food additives—sugar, sweeteners, dyes, salts, MSG, and caffeine—and can also lack a lot of the important nutrients that human bodies need to keep a balanced and healthy mental state. The following are a few examples of mood-improving chemicals that are missing from most processed foods.

Omega-3 fatty acids are one of the key ingredients that can be stripped out of processed foods, or skipped over in an unhealthy diet. These fats come mainly from fresh fish such as tuna, salmon, herring, trout, and sardines. Out of six double-blind tests examining the anti-depressant properties of omega oils, five tests showed that depressed patients who were dosed with these oils showed an average of 53 percent improvement in mood, and that the more oils consumed, the better the results were. Although research is still in progress, medical professionals suspect that omega oils help to build and maintain the cells and neurotransmitter receptors in the brain. If this is true, people with more omega-3 in their blood will be more likely to produce serotonin, and more likely to benefit from its effects.

B-vitamins, including B_2, B_3, B_6, B_{12}, and folic acid, are all closely related to mental health, and can be severely lacking from a diet composed of only processed foods. These vitamins, along with zinc, magnesium, and trimethylglycine (TMG), can help normalize the amino acid homocysteine, which is strongly linked to depression. Folic acid supplements have proven to increase the effectiveness of other depression medications by lowering homocysteine levels, and low homocysteine levels allow the brain to do a better job of self-regulating its chemical activity.

It has also been theorized that people with chronically low levels of vitamin B_1, also known as thiamine, may present with neurological symptoms, including drastic swings between hyperactivity and lethargy. Vitamin B_1 is necessary for the digestion of sugar, and the combination of large amounts of sugar with low levels of thiamine can make sugary processed foods hard to digest for the average person, leading to further mood swings and blood-sugar spikes.

Overall, it is important to remember that your body hasn't evolved to understand the processed foods that we consume today. Flooding your system with chemicals and additives that it doesn't understand is an easy way to stress out your system and set off your internal panic alarms or leave you feeling unsatisfied, which can lead to a whole host of new psychological and physiological problems. While you don't have to entirely revolutionize your diet, making sure to eat foods that are as close to their original form as possible is a great way to get the nutrients that you need without the fillers and harmful extras that can harmfully alter with your chemistry.

Food Sensitivities

While you may not be all-out allergic to certain foods or additives, sensitivities and intolerances to certain chemicals and compounds are very real for anxiety sufferers, and can cause physical reactions that range from digestive issues and irritability all the way to anxiety, moodiness, and depression.

Celiac Disease is a great example of such an issue. This disease presents as an inability of the small intestine to process gluten (a common protein found in wheat, rye, and barley, and almost all of the derivatives of these products), and results in inflammation, diarrhea, anemia, abdominal pain, and mouth ulcers. These issues can also lead to an accompanying lactose intolerance, which can further exacerbate these symptoms. In recent population studies, medical professionals have found that Celiac Disease can be associated with an 80 percent increase in risk for depressive behavior or clinical depression.

Because the reactions to food intolerances can be so diverse— from sleepiness and dizziness to gas and vomiting, all the way to chronic anxiety—it is much more difficult to diagnose these issues, especially in people who already present similar symptoms due to other illnesses. The best thing to do is keep track of what you eat, and notice if you see any changes in your mood or physical health in the next few hours. If you find that you always feel less than your best after eating a bowl of ice cream, try cutting dairy out of your diet for a few weeks; then deliberately add dairy back in to your diet and see the direct effect it has on your mood.

Detecting gluten intolerances can be the most difficult, as gluten can be found in so many places in today's culinary landscape that it can be very hard to avoid. Furthermore, because gluten molecules are so complex, they take a long while to escape the body, meaning that people who do cut gluten successfully out of their diet may not notice an improvement for several months. Before embarking on a gluten-free diet, be sure that you know exactly where gluten might be hiding, and be prepared to keep at it for a long while before you notice a difference.

Over-the-Counter and Prescription Medications

It is important to consider that each brain is unique, and there are many ingredients in medications, both prescribed and over-the-counter, that can interact negatively with our individual brain chemistry. Especially for people with anxiety, reading up on the active ingredients in your medications is a great way to make sure that your anxiety is under control, and isn't being sabotaged by unwanted chemical interference. Here are a few common ones to be aware of:

Pseudoephedrine is the active ingredient in all of the cold and allergy medications that are kept behind the counter. These medications are kept under close observation because they are commonly used to synthesize methamphetamines, which gives you a great clue about the possible negative effects of drugs containing pseudoephedrine. Its primary effects are nasal and sinus decongestion, but this comes along with the price of restlessness, nervousness, or overstimulation.

Dextromethorphan is a cough suppressant, and can be spotted in most brand-name medicines that include the letters "DM" in the name. This ingredient can cause restlessness, nervousness, and dizziness.

Antihistamines are chemicals that are used to tamp down your body's reaction to allergens and other irritations, and there are many different types that are used for many different specific treatments. The most common are included in products designed to relieve stuffy noses and sniffles, and in generic allergy medications. These chemicals generally have sedative properties, which is important to recognize before you start getting inexplicably tired, which may be one of your panic triggers.

Caffeine and other stimulants can be found in almost all weight loss medications, as well as in many migraine-specific painkillers, non-drowsy cold or allergy medications, decongestants, and asthma treatments. Keep an eye out for these stimulants, as they can increase your heart rate and exacerbate anxiety.

Norepinephrine and epinephrine, which we discussed earlier as the neurotransmitters that prepare your body for fight-or-flight responses, can also be found in nasal sprays. Avoid chemical sprays when your nose is stuffy, and stick with a plain saline solution if irrigation is needed.

Narcotic painkillers such as Percocet, Codeine, and Vicodin can deplete your endorphin system, causing rebound issues such as depression, pain, irritability and anger as soon as you stop taking them, which can lead to chemical dependency.

Adding these factors, and potential withdrawal symptoms, to existing anxiety disorders can be very dangerous.

Ibuprofen is one of the most common painkillers available on the market, but it has been known to exacerbate anxiety and depression. Steer clear of these types of painkillers and aim towards acetaminophen- or aspirin-based painkillers for your minor aches and pains.

Knowing what you are putting into your body is a great way to take control of your anxiety. Not only can you pick and choose the medications that will interfere least with your personal chemistry, but you can be informed of the symptoms that may arise when you do choose to take a certain medication, which will make for fewer worrying surprises later on.

Nicotine

While most people are aware of the physical risks of nicotine use, it is important to be aware of the mental effects of smoking and the consumption of other tobacco products, especially for people who have anxiety. Most smokers use tobacco as a form of self-medication, as nicotine creates an immediate sense of relaxation that can feel like relief from stress and anxiety.

Research into this process, however, has revealed that nicotine can actually increase anxiety and tension through a process called the rebound effect. After the immediate sensation of relaxation has passed, the nicotine user is left with his original stress and anxiety, and the added negative effects of nicotine withdrawal, such as headaches, breathlessness, anxiousness, and irritability. Smoking more may temporarily reduce these symptoms, but regular doses can permanently alter your brain chemistry and make you more dependent on nicotine in the long run, and can disrupt your brain's ability to remain stable on its own.

Alcohol

Alcohol is another substance that results in a rebound effect for people suffering from depression or anxiety, and while the alcohol itself is denatured and flushed from the human body within twelve hours, its effect on brain chemistry can last up to three months.

It has been estimated that up to 85 percent of alcoholics started drinking to self-medicate. This was certainly why I began to drink. For people who suffer from anxiety, depression, social phobias, or shyness, alcohol can seem to be an easy solution to get over discomfort at parties or in other social situations, or to numb anxiety and forget pain. Once the alcohol has stopped impairing their judgment processes, however, anxiety sufferers will find that the physical and chemical effects of alcohol have the opposite effect, and they will feel the need to drink more to suppress these further negative feelings.

There is a whole other unfortunate factor for persons abusing alcohol. Alcohol abuse results in a worse prognosis for a person with mental illness. People who are actively using alcohol are less likely to follow through with the treatment plans they created with their mental health professionals. They are less likely to adhere to their medication regimens and more likely to miss appointments, which leads to more psychiatric hospitalizations and other adverse outcomes. Active users are also less likely to receive adequate medical care for similar reasons and are more likely to experience severe medical complications and early death. People with mental illness who abuse alcohol are also at increased risk of impulsive and potentially violent acts. Perhaps most troubling and worrisome is that people who abuse alcohol are more likely to both attempt suicide and to die from their suicide attempts.

People with mental illness and active alcohol abuse are less likely to achieve lasting sobriety. They may be more likely to experience severe complications of their substance abuse, to end up in legal trouble from their substance use and to become physically dependent on alcohol. (For more information about the correlation between addiction and anxiety, see appendix three.)

Peace of Body, Peace of Mind

For those of us who live with mental illnesses such as anxiety, and are determined to life a life free from its bondage, it is especially important to monitor what chemicals and additives we are consuming as well as what nutrients we might be missing out on. If you feel sluggish or irritable after a meal, knowing what in your foods might have caused that issue can put your symptoms into perspective and help you make progress toward actively feeling better.

If you are not accustomed eating healthy, minimally-processed and augmented foods, pairing your doctor's medications with a more complete diet can improve your energy and outlook on life more effectively than a treatment plan alone. If your anxiety is rooted in nutrient deficiency or chemical toxicity, you may be able to work with your doctor to completely remove yourself from medications in time.

Taking stewardship of your body is a great way to feel in control of your life and your treatment, and it can be a big relief for those who are already prone to anxiety to know that they are doing their best to take care of their mind and their body.

Exercise and Anxiety

Today, almost everyone is aware of the importance of exercise for fitness and physical health. What is rarely emphasized, however, is how important exercise can be when it comes to taking care of the mind/body. While looking and feeling good can be a great boost for self-image and self-esteem, the chemical and physical changes that take place when you exercise can truly revolutionize your life, particularly if you are an anxiety sufferer.

There are a host of physical health problems that can come along with being out of shape, and these problems can lead to mental problems such as anxiety, as well as depression and insomnia. Exercise has an incredible effect on your physical well-being, which, in turn, affects your mental well-being. It is much easier to be happy when you feel safe and secure in your own body, and physical improvement can be a great source of pride and satisfaction for long-time sufferers of physical health issues such as diabetes and chronic pain and certainly anxiety.

Fitness and Body Chemistry

Keeping fit and eating right has a huge impact on your hormone and other chemical levels, which can make all the difference to how you feel both mentally and physically. Here are just a few of the chemicals that can change the way that you feel:

- *Testosterone*—While women only produce ten percent of the testosterone that men do, this hormone plays the same part for both sexes, increasing muscle strength, bone density, metabolism, and sexual desire. Too little testosterone can leave sufferers feeling tired and depressed. Losing weight and building strength is a good way to increase your body's testosterone levels, which will leave you feeling energetic and powerful.

- *Cortisol*—This chemical is a stress hormone that prepares your body for extreme circumstances by suppressing testosterone, speeding up the heart rate, increasing blood oxygen, and unleashing energy by burning fat. Reducing stress means that cortisol will also decrease, allowing testosterone to do its work. If you are constantly bogged down with stress, your body will give up and stop producing cortisol, and you will end up storing fat and constantly feeling tired. Bursts of intense exercise, usually under forty minutes, can lower cortisol levels and put your body back into sync.

- *Estrogen and Progesterone*—Although these hormones are typically thought of as being woman-only territory, they are equally important in both males and females. Increased estrogen levels can cause symptoms such as headaches, weight gain, fatigue, depression, and repressed libido in both genders, and progesterone exists to combat these effects. Because excess body fat secretes estrogen, keeping body fat levels low and eating healthy foods can keep these hormones balanced and your emotions in check.

- *Human Growth Hormone (hGH)*—This hormone promotes muscle growth and burns excess fat, and also plays an important part in living longer and generally feeling better. Exercise increases hGH levels, especially resistance training at high intensity.

The human body evolved in an environment where motion "fight or flight" were the keys to survival, and it has not caught up to today's sedentary lifestyles. Those powerful stress hormone chemicals like cortisol, which do such a good job for us when we need to "fight or flee," now just sit there in our bodies—unless, however, we do something, like exercise vigorously, to cause a natural excretion from our bodies. This is not only emotional stress-management, it is essential stress-chemical management!

Fitness, Anxiety, and Stress

Anxiety sufferers don't corner the market on stress. Stress is an issue that affects everyone, although some people are more susceptible to stress-related issues than others. Exercise has been found to reduce the effects of stress, and to decrease other factors that can lead to stress, such as lack of energy and feelings of physical illness. There are, however, more direct ways in which exercise may impact our ability to cope with stressful situations.

The newest studies reveal that physical activity can actually encourage new neurons to be created in the brain, especially in areas related to thinking, memory, and emotion. The creation of new, excitable neurons makes the brain more adaptable and receptive to new information. However, it's important to note that these new excitable neurons can lead to symptoms of anxiety. The good news for the regulation of those new neurons our brain creates from healthy moderate exercise is the brain compensates for this excitability factor. The brain also creates neurons that release and regulate a hormone called gamma-aminobutyric acid (GABA). GABA, which is the chemical targeted by most anti-anxiety drugs, limits the firing of the neurons and leads to a calmer mind. Scientists have noted that active animals far more of both the excitable and the calming neurons than sedentary creatures. The theory holds that while active creatures may be more likely to react quickly to a stressful situation, they may also be quicker to calm down afterwards.

Another potential danger with exercise is that the rapid buildup of lactic acid can also contribute to symptoms of anxiety. I had a personal experience with this. I decided, about three years into my recovery from anxiety, that I was going to get in shape! So, I promptly went to the track field at our local High School and ran a mile and half the first time out. The next couple of days at work I felt like I was on the verge of having a full-blown panic attack, and was really alarmed by this. I went straight to my psychiatrist and told him how I as feeling. He asked me if I had eaten anything different or changed any activity habits, so I told him about running the mile and half. He said, "Suzanne, did you ever think about building up to running a mile and half?" "No," I said. "Why?" Then he explained that anxiety sufferers are sensitive to the buildup of lactic acid in the muscles. Another lesson in moderation. And in moderation, exercise turns out to be critical. Keeping in shape has been an important part of my ongoing quest for peace of mind and mental wellness.

Studies find time and time again that animals who exercise more often, either by choice or by necessity, are more able to cope with stress and anxiety, and that these same results can be repeated in humans. People who exercise regularly are over 25 percent less likely to develop depression or anxiety in the future. Between the release of relaxing hormones and the physical satisfaction of exercise, channeling energy into physical fitness is a great way for anxiety sufferers to distract themselves from negative, often life-consuming symptoms, and to get relief from feelings of panic, worry, and fear, and for people who are bogged down from stress to avoid letting it consume them.

Fitness and Depression

Anxiety sufferers often also suffer from depression. And while a quick workout may not be able to cure depression or repair the underlying causes of depressive symptoms, studies as far in the past as 1981 show that regular exercise can help people with mild or moderate depression to improve their emotional state, and that physical activity may help to lessen the symptoms of severe depression when paired with an effective treatment program.

Studies show that people performing exercise instead of or in addition to their depression medication were found to recover from their depressive symptoms at the same rate as people who took medication alone. Although the depression medications were more effective immediately, patients who continued to exercise after the study were far less likely to relapse into depression after they had stopped taking their medication.

A full exercise regimen is a great thing, but don't discount the value in a good walk. Both can turn around feelings of weariness, unhappiness, and even aches and pains. Physical activity makes your brain release chemicals, most notably endorphins, which dull your feelings of pain and create a positive or euphoric feeling which can counteract the negative effects of depression, and frequent exercise can also limit or erase triggers for depression, such as stress, self-esteem issues, and chronic pain.

Fitness and Low Self-Esteem

We've talked earlier in this book about how a negative perception of our bodies can have an incredibly negative impact on our mental and physical health. While self-criticism can be a motivating drive to make positive change, over-criticizing oneself can lead to dangerous life choices, acceptance of emotional or physical abuse, and potentially the perpetration of violence against oneself or others. While moderate to severe self-esteem issues should be discussed with and treated by a physician, exercise and a healthy diet can be a great way for anyone suffering self-esteem issues to buff up their confidence levels.

First and foremost, exercise can help reduce the physical problems that cause the body image issue in the first place. While there is no magic cure for obesity or lack of muscle density, the safest and most effective way to gain the shape that you desire is to exercise regularly and eat healthy, nutritionally-balanced foods. Exercise doesn't need to be difficult or dedicated—simply setting aside thirty minutes a day for a walk or taking the stairs instead of the escalator can help to begin the process of shedding unwanted weight and training the body to be a calorie-burning machine.

It is also important to consider the mental impact of increased exercise. Not only does the exercise increase your happiness hormones, but the combination of positive chemicals and the satisfaction of progress can make all the difference to someone who struggles with their body image or self-esteem. Exacting change on your self is hard work, and seeing even the smallest of changes can make a big difference in your outlook on your power to change and improve yourself.

Fitness and Insomnia

Unfortunately insomnia is often a close companion for anxiety sufferers. Although scientists are still unsure how exactly exercise can aid in sleeping, it has been noted by sleep specialists all over the world that exercise can improve sleep duration and quality for many sufferers of insomnia and other sleeping disorders. There are several theories as to the exact mechanism of exercise-induced sleep, which include:

෴ **Body Heat** —The heating of your body during exercise, especially in the afternoon and evening hours, makes your body feel alert and prepared, while the subsequent cooling may result in drowsiness and comfortable sleep.

෴ **Anxiety and Depression**—Insomnia is often linked to these other illnesses, and the suppressive effects of exercise on the chemicals that cause their symptoms could lead to a better night's sleep.

෴ **Circadian Rhythms**—Because your body evolved to be awake and moving during the day and still and sleepy at night, any maladjustment of the internal clock can result in drowsiness during the day and sleeplessness at night. Exercising at the right points in the day may be able to trick your body clock back into the right rhythm and restore your ability to sleep at night.

෴ **Endorphins**—These and other chemicals produced by exercise have a sedative effect, allowing for people who struggle to sleep to fall asleep faster and stay asleep longer.

Good sleep habits and an adequate amount of sleep are so important for anxiety sufferers to reduce any sleep deprivation related anxiety symptoms. It is also necessary to promote both overall physical and mental well-being, so be sure to consult with a physician if you are experiencing any difficulty in sleeping or staying asleep, or if you find yourself to be consistently tired throughout the day.

Fitness, Low Energy, and Fatigue

Low energy and fatigue can often trigger a desire for a caffeinated boost, which is problematic for the anxiety sufferer. While it may sound counter-intuitive, a much better solution is to get up off that couch and exercise. I know may be the last thing you feel like doing when you are feeling fatigued or sluggish, but recent studies have found that exercise can have both short-term and long-term effects on energy levels. The important thing is that you do something. Just get started. Start by walking around the block and then give yourself permission to do it again.

This is how it works: exercise carries oxygen, water, and nutrients to your muscles, allowing them to make the chemical adenosine triphosphate, which is what the body recognizes as energy. This process is what converts the nutrients that you have consumed into usable energy, and prevents fats from being stored. The more muscle you have, and the more oxygen and water in your blood, the more energetic you will feel.

Researchers have found that even such little work as three twenty- to thirty-minute exercise sessions per week can feel less fatigued and more energized than peers who otherwise wouldn't exercise. These periods of activity can include such simple tasks as gardening or walking, and can extend up to cycling, swimming, and jogging for more established exercisers.

Fitness and Medication

Physical fitness is especially important for people who are being medicated, especially for those who are medicated for mental health issues. Many medications increase the risk for obesity, heart disease, high cholesterol, and diabetes, among other illnesses. Exercise can help reduce these risks, and being aware of your body can help you to detect these issues when they do arise.

Exercise can also be used to supplement medications, especially after the initial dosage. While prescription-strength chemicals may be needed to get your condition under control so that you can function, they may not be the only solution, and they may not be the complete solution that you would hope for in a medication. Exercise and other personal care can fill in the gaps where your medication leaves off and can make your recovery faster and longer lasting.

It is also important to remember that medications aren't a cure, especially for diseases such as anxiety and depression that can be caused or enhanced by underlying issues in your life. Medication cannot solve the roots of these problems, as outlined in this book. Neurogenesis Meditation Therapy, together with sleep, proper nutrition, and regular exercise, can be used to cure underlying problems, and these are solutions that will last once you and your doctor have decided that your medication is no longer necessary.

Community and Fitness

Being around other people and nurturing relationships outside family is rarely emphasized as an essential element in the recovery of mental illness. Yet I believe it needs to be right up there with meditation and medication. Fellowship is not only a spiritual experience; it is also, once again, a brain changer! Research shows that when we just watch two people hugging, there is a dramatic secretion of the feel-good hormone, dopamine, in our brains. Group exercise can be a great way to connect with others and a source of motivation for people who are just starting out their fitness journeys or for people who are bored of their current routine. At most fitness centers classes are offered for anyone from the newest beginner to the most seasoned exercise veteran.

Remember to keep an open mind when starting an exercise routine, and to relax and have fun, even though it may be hard. You may sweat up a storm and you may be sore the next day, but everyone in the group is there to make changes to themselves, too, and at the end of the day, you will all feel a lot better for having worked out together.

Substance Abuse and Addiction Resulting from Anxiety Disorders

Anxiety disorders can be debilitating and embarrassing, which is why only three-quarters of sufferers seek help according to the National Institute of Mental Health. Another reason is that many sufferers choose to self-medicate with drugs or alcohol or both, as was my case. New research is coming to light that posits that all addiction may result from a desire to self-medicate for a variety of painful or disturbing symptoms related to mental illness, including those caused by excessive anxiety.

It stands to reason that individuals suffering from anxiety disorders are twice as likely as the general population to suffer from addiction to illicit drugs or alcohol. Likewise those suffering with a substance use disorder are twice as likely to have a co-occurring anxiety disorder.

To compound the problem, anxiety sufferers are in general more likely to abuse a wide array of mind-altering substances, such as the class of drugs known as benzodiazepines, which include and are more commonly known as Valium, Xanax, Klonopin, and Ativan. Additionally, anxiety sufferers have a high prevalence of addiction to the opiate class (painkillers, heroin, etc.) because of their mental and physical numbing effects. Even cigarettes are more popular among those with anxiety disorders than in the general population.

Typically, interactions with these drugs are precipitated by the individual choosing to self-medicate in an effort to relieve the symptoms of her or his anxiety disorder. Addiction begins when the sufferer achieves a measure of relief from the symptoms, which sets up a pattern of self-medication and can lead to using more than one drug at a time. Over time, the individual builds a tolerance to the drugs or alcohol, leading to increased consumption and eventual addiction. The patterns of self-medicating are further complicated when individuals experience relief of anxiety while under the influence of their chosen drugs, alcohol for example; yet when the numbing effects wear off, the anxiety returns to a greater degree. This often leads to consuming even more of the drug in order to stave off the impending rebound effect of an increase in anxiety. As a result, this type of self-medication becomes a never-ending cycle of increasing drug use and eventual abuse.

Boredom and Stress as Root Causes of Addiction

People begin using drugs for different reasons. There are endless reasons as to why we pick up a drink or a drug in the first place. One of the most common reason people give is boredom. Drug and alcohol users often say that engaging in the use of their preferred addictive substances helps to alleviate feelings of boredom and makes passing time more enjoyable. In my experience, the word "boredom" is used when the real problem is actually more akin to lack of motivation, which also is accompanied by procrastination. Lack of motivation and procrastination bring with it a whole new dimension of stress, anxiety, and the need to self medicate. Boredom seems a little bit less responsible for the state of being rather than no motivation.

Individuals who appear to be are easily bored are considered more high-risk in the development of several disorders, including anxiety disorders, anger management problems, and depression. All of these disorders also increase an individual's risk of developing an addiction.

The use of drugs or alcohol to alleviate boredom is often thought to be recreational; however, the most common recreational drugs are also those with the highest addictive potential, including alcohol, cocaine, heroin, and prescription pain medications. What begins as recreational use quickly escalates into full-blown addiction simply because of the highly addictive nature of this class of drugs.

Aside from boredom (which I believe creates stress), stress is the most commonly cited factor in beginning to use or abuse drugs and alcohol. Stress is a normal, natural part of life, but as discussed in this book, the chronic stress experienced by some individuals in today's world can be debilitating.

I've presented a lot of mind-body ways to combat stress and manage anxiety in this book, but one of the most obvious ways to deal with a problematic source of stress is to evaluate solutions to abusive or problematic relationships, looking for a new source of income or putting oneself in a more favorable situation. Individuals who handle stress well use these types of coping mechanisms, but those who do not handle stress well may choose less effective methods of coping, including turning to drugs or alcohol, which may seem at first glance to be highly effective tools in fighting stress.

Alcohol and drugs trigger the release of naturally occurring brain chemicals that are related to relaxation and pleasure. The use of alcohol and drugs causes an over-production of these feel-good, pleasure-inducing hormones, which makes us crave them more. This is particularly true for persons suffering long-term chronic stress as opposed to sufferers of other types of stress.

In one recent study, researchers posited that a stressed brain releases a chemical called corticosterone. This chemical enhances the pleasure the brain feels in response to the stimulus of cocaine, leading to relatively low doses of the drug having a very large impact and priming the brain to fall into addiction much more quickly than a brain not suffering from excessive stress.[39]

Another recent study found in *Current Directions in Psychological Science* suggested that individuals with addictions may overcome them, only to be pulled back into addictive behavior patterns when under stress. The researchers further posited that the areas of the brain aroused by stress are the same areas of the brain aroused by drug use. During a stressful situation, an individual's brain may get a reminder of the effect of drugs and thereby demand drugs in response.[40]

How Stress and Boredom Affect Typical Addictions

The links between stress, boredom, and addiction are in the chemistry of the brain itself. Understanding how these links work is essential for individuals endeavoring to break the bonds of addiction. Stress and boredom can play major roles as triggers for relapse in individuals who have succeeded in recognizing and controlling their addiction. It is nearly impossible to find a case of addiction where the contributing factors were something other than stress or boredom.

Addicts attempting to recover from their addictions are often taken by surprise by how closely stress and boredom relate to their desire to begin using drugs or alcohol after successfully quitting.

Recovering addicts have been studied extensively to understand how these triggers work on various kinds of addictions, including addictions to sex, gambling, pornography, shopping, eating and others. Due to these studies, the link between stress, boredom, and addiction has long been established, albeit not well understood. Because the causation is obvious, stress management courses and other similar types of intervention have been recommended as part of the treatment for recovering addicts. In the field of addiction treatment, current research is pointing to medical interventions that may be more useful in helping an addict break the stress/boredom/addiction cycle.

As might be expected, the understanding of the psychology behind drug-seeking and addictive behavior is clearer than the neurology. Commonly abused drugs induce a profound sense of euphoria or relaxation for the user, making them useful, at least on a superficial level, for the relief of stress and boredom. A drink or two after work can unintentionally develop into a full-blown alcohol addiction, even though it began as a way to relax after a long day. Some individuals may decide to reward themselves after a tough week by going out to a club and using a little cocaine, heroin, or ecstasy in order to relieve the stress built up during the week. As the user begins to associate the use of drugs or alcohol with their relaxation, the efficacy of the substance for relieving stress and boredom becomes more pronounced and encourages psychological dependence before physical dependence becomes an issue.

Just from this little bit of information I've given you on stress and boredom, you can easily see how the unsuspecting casual user/drinker can easily lead to addiction. The user/drinker sees the drug as an answer to excessive stress and boredom, but since stress is a normal part of everyday life, addiction becomes more and more likely. Drugs and alcohol are seen by the user/drinker to be a useful way to relieve stress and alleviate boredom, but as the addiction progresses, the drugs become the problem, rather than the solution. Even if an individual has succeeded in not taking drugs for stress relief for an extended period, a particularly stressful event could cause them to return to their addictive behaviors.

Addiction Rehabilitation Therapies

If you have found yourself, as I did, with an unintended addiction as a result of attempting to manage your anxiety, you may find it hard or even impossible to break the cycle of addiction on your own. Don't beat yourself up for this. This is an extremely common unfortunate occurrence, so you're not alone. Participating in a chemical dependency or dual diagnosis treatment program can allow you to gain a better understanding of the situations that have led to your substance use and abuse and help you learn to manage it. Many hospitals and treatment centers are using therapies like Cognitive Behavioral Therapy, mindfulness-based meditation practice, and even hypnosis to help patients become aware of how stress and boredom can trigger relapse, as well as helping them to develop coping mechanisms which are more effective for dealing with stressors. This allows us to deal with our stress and anxiety in a more productive fashion, without the risk of falling back to using drugs or alcohol.

Daily Treatment Options for Anxiety Disorders and Stress Triggers

Outside of in-patient treatment options, daily changes to your routine can increase the likelihood of successful abstinence of drug or alcohol abuse. In a study reported in *Harvard Mental Health Letter*, researchers were able to verify that individuals under a great deal of stress were more likely to eat foods which were high in fat, sodium, and sugar, and to smoke cigarettes and be disinclined to exercise.[41] All of these factors contribute to an individual feeling unhealthy and more likely to suffer from anxiety disorders and resultant addiction.

Once therapy had begun, individuals who made lifestyle changes such as improving their diet, quitting smoking and beginning an exercise regimen were far more likely to achieve recovery from their addiction and reduce their stress and boredom triggers. As part of a complete recovery program, individuals who were encouraged to eat healthier foods, get more exercise, and make improvements in their overall daily routines experienced better results over the long term than individuals who only underwent therapeutic treatments. Such daily routine improvements resulted in the individual feeling less stress and boredom, leaving them better able to handle transient stressors.

Having a sense of community can again be an invaluable resource in dealing with stress and boredom. For individuals suffering from chronic stress, community programs were often essential to help them deal with long-term stressors and the underlying causes of chronic stress. Some of these stressors included daily activities such as grocery shopping, or more episodic situations such as needing to secure new living accommodations or interviewing for a job. Addiction treatment programs that collaborated with community-based programs were more helpful to individuals suffering from chronic stress than programs that dealt strictly with therapies because they were more effective in dealing with the roots of long-term, chronic stress.

Helping others is not only a great way to combat the stress of boredom; it also rebuilds self-esteem that had been lost to addiction. When individuals undertake an activity that directly benefits others, they may experience increased satisfaction with themselves and feel more in control of their own lives. Volunteering in a community outreach program and helping underprivileged individuals can provide a sense of euphoria and peacefulness. It can also help an individual have more energy, allowing the person to be more interested in outside endeavors. For individuals suffering from a drug or alcohol addiction, volunteering can be the difference between achieving recovery and suffering a relapse.

Avoiding the Dangers of Stress

The truth is that stress is at the root of nearly every addiction and contributes heavily to relapse in otherwise well-recovering individuals. When endeavoring to combat stress and anxiety issues, it's important to be proactive. Waiting until stress and anxiety strikes is a poor plan; the prevention of stress and anxiety is essential to an addict making a full recovery. Preventing these feelings is an effective way to prevent a relapse and helps an addicted individual to enjoy life more fully and stay motivated.

Individuals who engage in activities that are sufficiently stimulating are less likely to experiment with addictive substances, meaning that these individuals are less likely to become addicted or fall into addictive thought and behavior patterns. Without such stimulating activities, the chances of becoming addicted to illicit substances increases by orders of magnitude.

In a study involving more than 350 addicted individuals who had successfully completed a rehabilitation program, stress and anxiety were the number one reasons for relapsing back into drug and alcohol abuse. These were closely followed by loneliness, anger, and boredom. Many addicted individuals in the study stated that without their drug of choice, they felt empty and lost.[42] This is why it is so important to treat anxiety disorders and their resultant addictions in a comprehensive way that includes overall lifestyle changes and therapy.

Planning for Your Recovery

Countless studies have come to the conclusion that just going through withdrawal is not an effective strategy for dealing with addiction, mainly because of the correlation between stress, anxiety, boredom, and addiction. Without an overall plan to combat these factors, an addicted individual is unlikely to make a full recovery. If you tend to self-medicate with drugs and alcohol, it's critical to develop pursuits that increase your enjoyment of life and are more enjoyable when undertaken while sober. Remember, stress and anxiety are epidemic in the 21st century, and it's a natural response for sufferers to seek relief through whatever means are available. For those of us who eventually become alcoholics or addicts, it's never intentional. Again, you're not alone, and your fear of getting help is just a fear. The only thing to fear is the fear itself. If in-patient treatment becomes an option for you, I suggest ignoring your fear and taking full advantage of the opportunity to rediscover yourself, recover, and reclaim emotional health.

Notes

1 The Mayo Clinic, Panic Attacks and Panic Disorder: http://www.
mayoclinic.org/diseases-conditions/panic-attacks/basics/definition/
con-20020825, accessed August 2014.

2 Dan Harris, *10% Happier: How I Tamed the Voice in my Head, Reduced
Stress Without Losing My Edge, and Found Self-Help That Actually
Worked* (It Books, New York, 2014) pp. 1–2.

3 R. C. Kessler et al., "Prevalence and Effects of Mood Disorders on
Work Performance in a Nationally Representative Sample of U.W.
Workers," The American Journal of Psychiatry 163 (2006): 1561–
68.

4 "Prevalence and Incidence Studies of Anxiety Disorders: A Systematic
Review of the Literature," *The Canadian Journal of Psychiatry*, 51
(2006); pp. 100–13.

5 Paul J. Rosch, M.D., F.A.C.P, "Job Stress: America's Leading Adult
Health Problem," in *USA* Magazine, May 1991.

6 Bernie Siegel, M.D., *Love, Medicine, and Miracles* (William Morrow
Paperbacks, 1998) p. 69.

7 Scott Stossel, *My Age of Anxiety*, (Knopf, 2014) p. 12.

8 Anthony P. Winston, Elizabeth Hardwick and Neema Jaberi,
"Neuropsychiatric effects of caffeine" in *Advances in Psychiatric
Treatment* (2005) 11: pp. 432–439.

9 Stephen R. Covey, *The Seven Habits of Highly Effective People: Powerful
Lessons in Personal Change* (Free Press: 2004) p. 28.

10 Dan Harris, *10% Happier: How I Tamed the Voice in my Head, Reduced
Stress Without Losing My Edge, and Found Self-Help That Actually
Worked* (It Books, New York, 2014) p. xiv.

11 National Institute for Complementary and Alternative Medicine
(NICAM), http://nccam.nih.gov/health/meditation/overview.htm,
accessed August 2014.

12 The David Lynch Foundation, http://www.davidlynchfoundation. org/schools.html, accessed August 2014.

13 S.W. Lazar, C.E. Kerr, R.H. Wasserman, J.R. Gray, D.N. Greve, M.T. Treadway, M. McGarvey, B.T. Quinn, J.A. Dusek, H. Benson, S.L. Rauch, C.I. Moore, B. Fischl, 2005. "Meditation experience is associated with increased cortical thickness," *Neuroreport* 16 (17), 1893–1897.

14 Christopher Bergland, "How Does Meditation Reduce Anxiety at a Neural Level?" *Psychology Today online,* June 2006, http://www. psychologytoday.com/blog/the-athletes-way/201306/how-does-meditation-reduce-anxiety-neural-level, accessed August 2014.

15 S. Billioti de Gage, B. Bégaud, F. Bazin, H. Verdoux, J.F. Dartigues, K Pérès, T. Kurth, A. Pariente, "Benzodiazepine use and risk of dementia: prospective population based study" (September 2012). *BMJ* 345.

16 Herbert Benson, from his website http://www.relaxationresponse. org, accessed August 2014.

17 Jon Kabat-Zinn, *Wherever You Go, There You Are* (Hyperion; January 5, 2005) p.4.

18 Bethruth Naprastek, "What Is Guided Imagery?" on Health Journeys website, 2000: https://www.healthjourneys.com/WhatIsGuided Imagery, accessed August 2014.

19 ibid.

20 Mayo Clinic, "Enhance Healing Through Guided Imagery." ScienceDaily, 7 January 2008, www.sciencedaily.com/releases/2008/ 01/080104123246.htm, accessed August 2014.

21 ASCH website: http://www.asch.net/Public/GeneralInfoonHypnosis/ DefinitionofHypnosis.aspx, accessed August 2014.

22 National Alliance on Mental Illness, Treatments and Services: http:// www.nami.org/Content/NavigationMenu/Inform_Yourself/About_ Mental_Illness/About_Treatments_and_Supports/Cognitive_ Behavioral_Therapy1.htm, accessed August 2014.

23 Melody Beattie, *Codependent No More* (Hazelden; 2nd Revised edition, September 1, 1986) p. 31.

24 Brené Brown, *The Gifts of Imperfection: Let Go of Who You Think You're Supposed to Be and Embrace Who You Are* (Hazelden; 1 edition, 2010) p. 57.

25 ibid, p. 56.

26 Etienne Benson, "The Many Faces of Perfection," *Monitor on Psychology,* November 2003, Vol. 34, No. 10, p. 18.

27 Smedes, Louis, *The Art of Forgiving* (Ballantine Books; Fifth Printing edition, 1997) p. 12.

28 ibid, p. 6.

29 ibid, p. 137.

30 Charles Darwin, *The Expression of the Emotions in Man and Animals* (1872), published on Darwin Online, http://darwin-online.org.uk/content/frameset?pageseq=1&itemID=F1142&viewtype=text, Accessed August 2014.

31 John Bradshaw, *Bradshaw on the Family* (HCI; Revised edition, 1990) p. 3.

32 The Mayo Clinic, Agoraphobia: http://www.mayoclinic.org/diseases-conditions/agoraphobia/basics/definition/con-20029996, Accessed August 2014.

33 Alcoholics Anonymous, *The Big Book* (Alcoholics Anonymous World Services, 4th edition, 2002) p. 417.

34 Warren, Rick, *The Purpose Driven Life,* (Zondervan; Expanded edition, 2013) p. 182.

35 Joyce Meyer, *Battlefield of the Mind* (Warner Faith; Revised edition, 2002) p. 50.

36 Criteria for Alcohol Abuse can be found at the National Institute on Alcohol Abuse and Alcoholism, http://pubs.niaaa.nih.gov/publications/dsmfactsheet/dsmfact.pdf, accessed August 2014.

37 This version of the Two Wolves legend comes from First People: Native American Legends, http://www.firstpeople.us/FP-Html-Legends/TwoWolves-Cherokee.html, accessed August 2014.

38 Deepak Chopra, "What Is A Mantra?" on http://www.chopra.com/ccl-meditation/21dmc/mantra.html, accessed August 2014.

39 Richard J. Contrada and Andrew Baum, ed., *The Handbook of Stress Science: Biology, Psychology, and Health,* (Springer Publishing Company, 2011).

40 Nick E. Goeders, "Stress, Motivation, and Drug Addiction," *Current Directions in Psychological Science*, February 2004 13: 33–35.

41 "Why Stress Causes People to Overeat," *Harvard Mental Health Letter,* February 2012, http://www.health.harvard.edu/newsletters/harvard_mental_health_letter/2012/february/why-stress-causes-people-to-overeat, accessed September 2014.

42 Jane St. Clair, "Boredom and Substance Abuse: A Dangerous Combination," CRC Health Group, http://www.crchealth.com/addiction/drug-addiction-rehab/drug-addiction-rehab-2/home-2/drug_addiction/boredom-substance-abuse-a-dangerous-combination/, accessed Sept. 2014.

Index

About the Author

Rachel Holland Photography

Suzanne Jessee, M.A., C.Ht., is the creator of Escape Anxiety, a multi-disciplinary therapeutic program for the prevention, management, and treatment of anxiety and panic disorders. Using these techniques, Suzanne has been helping people attain physical relief and emotionally heal at leading chemical-dependency and dual-diagnosis treatment centers for the past decade. She conceived and built the anxiety-treatment specialty programs at the Betty Ford Center and Brighton Hospital, and is now dedicated to making excellent mental healthcare available to the public through her online programs, her book, her speaking engagements, and her TV appearances.

Suzanne earned her M.A. in Addiction Studies at the world-renowned Hazelden chemical-dependency treatment center in Center City, Minnesota, and her B.S. in psychology at Eastern Michigan University. She was trained and certified by the legendary Dr. Anna Spencer from the International Medical and Dental Hypnotherapy Association. Her unique contribution to anxiety treatment has been recognized by leaders in the field, including best-selling author Dr. Bernie Siegel.

Suzanne's journey to understand and cure anxiety disorders began when she was hospitalized in 1991 with severe depression, panic disorder, and early stages of agoraphobia. In addition, she struggled with alcoholism, as is common to anxiety sufferers. Since that day, it became her life's mission first to get well, and then to study the psychology and physiology of anxiety and panic disorders. Suzanne lives in Palm Desert, CA, with her miniature Chihuahua, Mr. Beasley. She enjoys cardio and nature hikes in the Coachella Valley Mountains with her daughter Breanna and Grandson, Grason. To escape the heat of the desert, she loves weekend getaways to Big Bear, Arrowhead, and the beautiful California coastline.